5-INGREDIENT
Freezer
MEALS

**65 SCRUMPTIOUS FREEZER MEALS
WITH 5 INGREDIENTS OR LESS**

ERIN CHASE

Published by FreezEasy Media, via CreateSpace.

ISBN 13: 9798703828212

For general information about our workshops, products and services, or to obtain technical support, please contact our Customer Care Team at support@freezeasy.com.

For more great recipes and resources, visit www.myfreezeasy.com.

FREE ONLINE WORKSHOP

Want to spend less time in the kitchen, and more time enjoying other things in life? Need dinner to "take care of itself"? Want to personalize and customize a freezer meal plan - with recipes your family will love?

MyFreezEasy will do all the heavy lifting for you! In a matter of seconds, our apps will pull together your freezer meal recipes, shopping lists, step-by-step instructions and printable labels for your meals. Load up your freezer with make-ahead meals and dinnertime will be a breeze.

In this free online workshop, you'll learn just about everything you need to know about freezer cooking and how it can transform your family's dinner experience.

Sign up for free at: www.myfreezeasy.com/workshop

TABLE OF CONTENTS

How Freezer Cooking
Helps Me Survive This Busy Mom Life

Freezer cooking and the "fast food at home" philosophy of MyFreezEasy has saved me from the drive thru - take out - dining out temptation on dozens (hundreds!?) of occasions! I'm not opposed to the drive thru or take out or dining out, but I do think those meals out on the town should be planned and part of your budget. Getting meals that hold up in the freezer and cook easily has helped keep me out of the drive thru and eating more meals at home that are healthier and more frugal.

Recently, I found myself at the pediatrician's office with the last appointment of the day. I generally have a 'no last appointment of the morning or afternoon' policy with doctor's offices, because you end up waiting while they catch up from falling behind throughout their visits. But that was the only slot I could get that day, for a son whom I suspected had strep throat.

I was still sitting in the waiting room at 4:50pm, waiting to see the doctor. At that point, I knew it would be 6pm before we got home, and I'm normally in the kitchen from 5 - 6pm to prep dinner or cook a freezer meal. That particular day, I was starting to worry. The temptation to hit the local burger joint on my way home was getting stronger. And just as I was adding up what that drive thru bill might cost, my husband texted that he was on his way home from work.

PHEW! I quickly texted back and asked if he'd be able to get dinner going in the skillet. He said he didn't have anything pressing when he got home, so I shot back the play-by-play on how to thaw and heat up some sloppy joe meat from the freezer.

When I finally arrived home after the strep test (it was positive) and buzzing through to pick up the prescription, it was 6pm. And it smelled amazing in the house, and I just scooped together some sloppy joes, cut up some fruit, grabbed some chips and dinner was served. Total cost of the meal was probably around $5-$6 for all of us. (I'm a ninja sales and deals grocery shopper!)

I was able to save dinner that night, without having to spend $45 in the drive thru!

Another example comes from a recent flu season. In 2018, the flu season was exceptionally rough and it hit our family twice - once with each strain. We ended up having a sick kid home from school and activities for 7 weeks in a row, with a brief reprieve in between the 2 strains.

I did my best to keep the sick ones quarantined, keep the house clean and disinfected, plus the time and energy spent nursing them back to health - I was exhausted. There was little energy left for dinner.

It was during those weeks that we'd have back-to-back-to-back freezer meals because they require little thought and little time and little energy to get onto the table.

Another great way to make freezer to slow cooker meals work in your favor is to take a peek at your weekly schedule and figure out which day or days you need help with dinner, or which days you have activities and appointments that keep you away from home and out of the kitchen from 5-6pm, when you would otherwise be doing meal prep. Make those your "standing freezer to slow cooker meal days."

For the past two years, our third son has a 5pm every Monday appointment with the occupational therapist. Her office is about a 20 minute drive, so we are away from home from 4:30ish to 6:30ish every Monday. I'm unable to be home, in the kitchen making a 'fresh meal' for dinner, so I let the slow cooker do the hard work for me. Every-single-Monday. Without fail.

Freezer meals and specifically "freezer to slow cooker meals" play such an important role in a busy mom's kitchen. They help keep dinner on the table night after night, even when life is busy, fast, hectic and chaotic. It's such a blessing having freezer meals "on backup" for the nights when you need them.

They also help you stay "one step ahead" with both the prepping and the cooking. This helps keep me balanced in my mental energy, eliminating the 'what's for dinner' question, plus it helps keep me on schedule with getting dinner on the table. It's so much easier for me to punch busy in the face when I have dinner "on demand" in the freezer.

Again, the idea and goal of these types of meals is to prepare make-ahead meals and keep them in your freezer, to heat or cook them quickly at a later time. My preferred method is to double 5 recipes, which gets me 10 meals into the freezer in one session. I have built the MyFreezEasy recipes, web app and mobile apps to reflect this philosophy and strategy.

Because it really is the easiest and best way to do "fast food at home."

Before we get to the recipes, I thought I'd share some other freezer cooking hacks with you.

Freezer Cooking Tips and Tricks

MyFreezEasy's freezer cooking meal plans are the perfect solution for the crazy busy home chef who wants to have less stress and less mess when getting dinner on the table.

MyFreezEasy meal plans are designed to help you get 10 meals into your freezer in under one hour, using recipes that can quickly be pulled together into freezer bags or trays. Yes, you can easily put together 10 "dump dinners" in an hour's time.

Even with the fast assembly process and cutting out the dinner hour stress, there are still a number of other essential "hacks" for putting together MyFreezEasy recipes and meal plans.

1. Let the food cool down completely to reduce risk of freezer burn!

2. Package up and remove as much air as possible, if using a plastic baggie. If using a plastic container and freezing liquid, be sure to leave enough headspace at the top, as the liquid will expand as it freezes.

3. "Flat freeze" by pressing the food as flat as possible in the baggie. Then you can stack meals and save space in your freezer. Place a piece of wax or parchment paper in between the baggies to prevent them from sticking together and tearing.

4. Thaw food completely in the fridge overnight or for up to 2 days if it is 'thick.' If you need the food that day, or within 30 minutes, you can let it soak in a warm bowl of water and it will quickly thaw. The thickness of the baggie or container will determine how long it will take to thaw. When I 'quick-thaw' things, it can take anywhere from 20 minutes to an hour.

Note: If utilizing the quick thaw method, please don't leave raw meat out on the counter in a bowl of warm water. Always let raw meat thaw in the refrigerator to keep it at proper cold temperatures.

5. My recommended "stay in the freezer times" are: up to 6 months for regular fridge freezer, or up to 12 months in deep freezer.

6. Do not (I repeat, do NOT!) shop and prep on the same day. Find a time in your schedule that will allow you to shop the day before, then prep the meals the following day.

7. When meat is on sale at your store, prepare the meals with a plan that will use up all the meat and you'll kill two birds with one stone. Then you will have saved a ton of:

- Money by stocking up on meat that is on sale.
- Time and sanity by prepping it all for dinner at once.

8. Use the "Prep Day Shopping List by Recipe" (within the MyFreezEasy Freezer Meal Plan) when in the checkout lane (or even as you are loading and unloading your cart!) to organize ingredients into specific bags so that when you get home, the ingredients are already grouped together by recipe. The

bagger might look at you like you've lost your mind, but you'll be smiling when you get home when it's already organized for your prep & assembly!

9. Drop produce and meats into the fridge in their bags so they are easy to pull out the next day when it's prep time. Leave shelf stable ingredients on the counter, ideally organized in their bags, to make prep set up a cinch.

10. Side Dishes: I leave these very much open and flexible to allow your family to decide which veggies and/or starches are best for your preferences. Make the most of sales and deals on produce and bulk rice or pasta to save big on side dishes too.

The Rules about
Erin's 5-Ingredient Freezer Meals

Throughout this cookbook, you will find meals that can be put together for the freezer using just 5-ingredients.

I wanted to outline and detail my definition of a 5-Ingredient Freezer Meal, as well as share a handful of exceptions.

First, the 5 ingredient count is based on the core ingredients that are being prepared into the freezer meals. Essentially that means that I don't include side dishes into the ingredient count. This would also mean that garnishes or toppings aren't included in the ingredient count.

Also, here's a short list of other items that I didn't include in the counts:

- Water
- Salt
- Pepper
- Garlic powder or minced onions (with ground beef recipes)
- Olive oil

Those are common enough ingredients that should appear in every kitchen, hence why I didn't include them in the total ingredient counts for each recipe.

I also don't include "accessories" like the disposable foil trays, gallon size freezer baggies, foil or parchment paper in the totals. Those items should be in the home of any home chef who is regularly making freezer meals.

All this to say...please don't email me if there's 1-2 of these extras, sides or garnishes that bump the grand total of ingredients over the number 5.

One final ingredient note: the average pounds for "4 small boneless, skinless chicken breasts" is about 1 ¼ to 1 ½ lbs. Grocery stores pack their chicken differently, so be on the lookout for about that many pounds. You could also choose to portion your chicken as 1 small chicken breast or 2 chicken thighs per person.

How to Best Use This Cookbook

This cookbook is a collection of simple, yet delicious recipes that will be fast to put together because of the minimal ingredient lists.

There are 65 recipes, broken up into four chapters. Each chapter contains recipes for chicken, beef, pork or seafood. The recipes are all clearly titled with the cooking method as well. This will make it easy for you to find specific recipes.

Finally, at the end of the recipe section there are two complete MyFreezEasy Freezer Meal Plans. Each plan contains five recipes that double to make ten freezer meals in one prep session. Each plan includes recipes, shopping lists, and step by step freezer meal prep assembly instructions, as well as thaw and cook instructions.

I strategically chose recipes of all the same meat type for the two freezer meal plans. The first one is all chicken recipes and the second one is all ground beef recipes. I chose these two meats because they are often on sale at the grocery store, and are two of the most common meats in many budget friendly, family friendly meals.

The goal with an "all the same meat type" freezer meal plan is to help you save as much money as you can at the grocery store. Meat is often the most expensive part of any meal, so when you can get 10 meals made with meat that is on sale, you'll start to see big savings on your grocery bill.

Next time you see boneless, skinless chicken breasts and ground beef on sale at your local grocery store, buy extra packages and then prep the meals in these two freezer meal plans. You'll enjoy savings at the store, as well as savings in time and your sanity.

With that, let's move onto the delicious recipes and freezer meal plans!

Chapter 1 –
5-Ingredient Chicken Recipes

Baked Basil Balsamic Chicken
Baked Pesto Chicken
Baked Sweet Chili Chicken
Grilled Garlic Lime Chicken
Grilled Honey Mustard Chicken
Slow Cooker Apricot Chicken
Slow Cooker BBQ Chicken Street Tacos
Slow Cooker Best Shredded Chicken Tacos
Slow Cooker Buffalo Chicken Nachos
Slow Cooker Baja Shredded Chicken Tacos
Slow Cooker Enchilada Chicken
Slow Cooker Garlic Parmesan Chicken
Slow Cooker Margarita Chicken
Slow Cooker Pepperoni Chicken
Slow Cooker Ranch Chicken Tacos
Slow Cooker Ranchero Chicken
Slow Cooker Shredded Hawaiian Chicken Sandwiches
Slow Cooker Thai Peanut Chicken
Sweet Potato Chicken Sausage Hash

Baked Basil Balsamic Chicken

Yield:	4 servings
Prep Time:	15 minutes*
Cook Time:	60 minutes

Ingredients

- 4 small boneless, skinless chicken breasts
- 1/2 cup balsamic vinegar
- 2 Tbsp olive oil
- Salt and pepper
- 2 tsp dried basil
- Side: rice
- Side: veggies
- 1 gallon-size freezer baggie

Cooking Directions

1. Place the chicken into a bowl or shallow dish and add the balsamic vinegar and olive oil. Season lightly with salt and pepper. *Let marinate in the fridge for at least 30 minutes, or overnight ideally.
2. Preheat the oven to 350 F. Lightly grease a 9x13-inch baking dish with non-stick cooking spray.
3. Place the marinated chicken in the baking dish and generously sprinkle the basil on top of the chicken. Bake in the preheated oven for 60 minutes, or until the chicken has cooked through. Cooking time may vary depending on the thickness of the chicken. Slice the chicken before serving.
4. Serve Basil Balsamic Chicken with rice and veggies.

Prepare to Freeze Directions

To a gallon-size plastic freezer baggie, add the following ingredients:
- 4 small boneless, skinless chicken breasts
- 1/2 cup balsamic vinegar
- 2 Tbsp olive oil
- Salt and pepper
- 2 tsp dried basil

Remove as much air as possible and seal. Add label to baggie and freeze.

Freeze & Thaw Directions

Put the baggie in the freezer and freeze for up to 6 months in a fridge freezer or 12 months in a deep freezer. Thaw completely in the fridge overnight, before transferring to the baking dish and baking as directed.

If baking from frozen or partially frozen, keep the dish covered tightly with foil and double the baking time. Bake until meat is cooked through.

Baked Pesto Chicken

Yield: 4 servings
Prep Time: 10 minutes
Cook Time: 60 minutes

Ingredients

- 4 small boneless, skinless chicken breasts
- Salt and pepper
- 8 oz. jar pesto
- 15 oz. can diced tomatoes
- 1 Tbsp Italian seasoning
- 2 cups shredded mozzarella cheese
- Garnish: fresh basil
- Side: salad
- Side: pasta
- 9x13-inch disposable foil tray

Cooking Directions

1. Preheat the oven to 400 F.
2. Place the chicken breasts into a 9x13-inch baking dish and sprinkle with a little salt and pepper. Spread a dollop of pesto onto each chicken breast. Pour the diced tomatoes over the top of all the chicken, then sprinkle the Italian seasoning over the top. Sprinkle the shredded mozzarella cheese on top.
3. Bake in the preheated oven for 50 to 60 minutes, or until chicken is cooked through. Cooking time may vary depending on the thickness of the chicken.
4. Prepare the salad.
5. Prepare the pasta as directed on the package.
6. Serve Pesto Chicken Bake over pasta with salad.

Prepare to Freeze Directions

Open 1 can of diced tomatoes.

To the disposable tray, add the following ingredients:
- 4 small boneless, skinless chicken breasts
- Salt and pepper
- Dollop of pesto to each chicken
- 15 oz. can diced tomatoes
- 1 Tbsp Italian seasoning
- 2 cups shredded mozzarella cheese

Cover tightly with foil or lid, add label to tray and freeze.

Freeze & Thaw Directions

Put the tray in the freezer and freeze for up to 6 months in a fridge freezer or 12 months in a deep freezer. Thaw in the fridge overnight, before transferring to the oven and baking as directed.

If baking from frozen or partially frozen, keep the dish covered tightly with foil and double the baking time. Bake until meat is cooked through.

Baked Sweet Chili Chicken

Yield:	4 servings
Prep Time:	10 minutes
Cook Time:	55 minutes

Ingredients

- 4 small boneless, skinless chicken breasts
- Salt and pepper
- 1 cup sweet Thai chili sauce
- 3 Tbsp soy sauce
- Side: rice
- Side: veggies
- 9x13-inch disposable foil tray

Cooking Directions

1. Preheat the oven to 400 F. Place the chicken breasts into a 9x13-inch baking dish and season with salt and pepper.
2. In a small mixing bowl, whisk together the sweet Thai chili sauce and soy sauce. Pour over the top of the chicken, and spoon any that falls off the chicken, back on top. The sauce will glaze onto the chicken as it bakes, so you want the chicken covered on top by the sauce.
3. Bake in the preheated oven for 50 to 55 minutes, or until chicken is cooked through.
4. Cook the rice, as directed.
5. Prepare the veggies.
6. Serve Baked Sweet Chili Chicken with rice and veggies.

Prepare to Freeze Directions

In a small mixing bowl, whisk together 1 cup sweet Thai chili sauce and 3 Tbsp soy sauce.

To the disposable tray, add the following ingredients:
- 4 small boneless, skinless chicken breasts
- Salt and pepper onto the chicken
- Prepared sauce/marinade, directly on the chicken

Cover with foil or lid, add label and freeze.

Freeze & Thaw Directions

Put the tray in the freezer and freeze for up to 6 months in a fridge freezer or 12 months in a deep freezer. Thaw in the fridge overnight, or a bowl of lukewarm water for about 20 minutes, before transferring to the oven and baking as directed.

If baking from frozen or partially frozen, keep the dish covered tightly with foil and double the baking time. Bake until meat is cooked through.

Grilled Garlic Lime Chicken

Yield:	4 servings
Prep Time:	10 minutes*
Cook Time:	16 minutes

Ingredients

- 4 small boneless, skinless chicken breasts
- 1/4 cup lime juice
- 1/4 cup olive oil
- 1 Tbsp minced garlic
- Salt and pepper
- Side: rice
- Side: salad
- 1 gallon-size freezer baggie

Cooking Directions

1. In a mixing bowl, whisk together the lime juice, olive oil, minced garlic, salt and pepper. Add the chicken breasts and coat with the marinade. *Place in the fridge and let marinate for at least 2 hours.
2. Preheat the grill.
3. Grill chicken breasts for 6 to 8 minutes per side, or until cooked through. Cooking time may vary depending on the thickness of the chicken. Discard excess marinade.
4. Cook the rice, as directed.
5. Prepare the salad.
6. Serve Grilled Garlic Lime Chicken over rice with salad.

Prepare to Freeze Directions

To a gallon-size plastic freezer baggie, add the following ingredients:
- 4 small boneless, skinless chicken breasts
- 1/4 cup lime juice
- 1/4 cup olive oil
- 1 Tbsp minced garlic
- Salt and pepper

Remove as much air as possible and seal. Add label to baggie and freeze.

Freeze & Thaw Directions

Put the baggie in the freezer and freeze for up to 6 months in a fridge freezer or 12 months in a deep freezer. Thaw completely in the fridge overnight before grilling. Transfer the chicken to grill, and grill as directed. Discard excess marinade.

Grilled Honey Mustard Chicken

Yield: 4 servings
Prep Time: 10 minutes*
Cook Time: 16 minutes

Ingredients

- 4 small boneless, skinless chicken breasts
- 1/4 cup honey
- 1/4 cup spicy mustard
- 2 Tbsp olive oil
- 1 Tbsp red wine vinegar
- Side: garlic bread
- Side: salad
- 1 gallon-size freezer baggie

Cooking Directions

1. In a small mixing bowl, whisk together the honey, spicy brown mustard, olive oil, and red wine vinegar. Whisk well to create a marinade.
2. Place the chicken breasts into a shallow baking dish or plastic baggie and pour the marinade over the top. Cover with plastic wrap or seal, and marinate in the fridge for at least 1 hour, but ideally overnight.*
3. Preheat the grill and add the marinated chicken breasts over the direct heat. Brush the top with the marinade, and discard remaining marinade. Let cook for 6 to 8 minutes per side, then move over indirect heat and grill until cooked through. Slice before serving.
4. Prepare the salad.
5. Prepare the garlic bread.
6. Serve Grilled Honey Mustard Chicken with salad and garlic bread.

Prepare to Freeze Directions

In a small mixing bowl, whisk together 1/4 cup honey, 1/4 cup spicy brown mustard, 2 Tbsp olive oil, and 1 Tbsp red wine vinegar. Whisk well to create a marinade.

To a gallon-size plastic freezer baggie, add the following ingredients:
- 4 small boneless, skinless chicken breasts
- Prepared sauce/marinade, directly on the chicken

Remove as much air as possible and seal. Add label to baggie and freeze.

Freeze & Thaw Directions

Put the baggie in the freezer and freeze for up to 6 months in a fridge freezer or 12 months in a deep freezer. Thaw completely in the fridge overnight, before transferring to the grill and grilling as directed and until cooked through. Discard excess marinade.

Slow Cooker Apricot Chicken

Yield: 4 servings
Prep Time: 10 minutes
Cook Time: 6 hours in the slow cooker

Ingredients

- 6 boneless, skinless chicken thighs
- 8 oz. jar apricot preserves
- 1/2 cup French salad dressing
- 2 Tbsp minced onion
- 1 tsp garlic powder
- Salt and pepper
- Side: dinner rolls
- Side: veggies
- 1 gallon-size freezer baggie

Cooking Directions

1. Place the chicken thighs into the base of the slow cooker.
2. In a small mixing bowl, combine the apricot preserves, French dressing, minced onion and garlic powder. Pour over top of the chicken in the slow cooker. Season with a little salt and pepper over the top.
3. Set on low and cook for 6 hours. (Note: if you wish to cook on low for 8 hours, add 1/2 cup water or chicken stock to the sauce.)
4. Warm dinner rolls.
5. Prepare veggies.
6. Serve Slow Cooker Apricot Chicken with dinner rolls and veggies.

Prepare to Freeze Directions

Whisk together 1 cup apricot preserves, 1/2 cup French dressing, 2 Tbsp minced onion, 1 tsp garlic powder and a few pinches of salt and pepper.

To a gallon-size plastic freezer baggie, add the following ingredients:
- 6 boneless, skinless chicken thighs
- Salt and pepper
- Prepared sauce/marinade, directly on the chicken

Remove as much air as possible and seal. Add label and freeze.

Freeze & Thaw Directions

Put the baggie in the freezer and freeze for up to 6 months in a fridge freezer or 12 months in a deep freezer. Thaw in the fridge overnight, or a bowl of lukewarm water for about 20 minutes, before transferring to a slow cooker and cooking on low for 6 hours.

If slow cooking from frozen or partially frozen, add ½ cup of water or chicken stock to the slow cooker insert and change the slow cook time to low for 8 hours.

Slow Cooker BBQ Chicken Street Tacos

Yield: 4 servings
Prep Time: 10 minutes
Cook Time: 8 hours in slow cooker

Ingredients

- 4 small boneless, skinless chicken breasts
- 2 cups BBQ sauce
- 15 oz. can black beans
- 1 small red onion
- 12 corn tortillas
- Garnish: shredded cheddar cheese
- Garnish: chopped cilantro
- Side: fruit
- 1 gallon-size freezer baggie

Cooking Directions

1. Chop the red onion.
2. Open, drain and rinse the can of black beans.
3. Spray bottom of slow cooker with cooking spray. Add the chicken breasts, black beans, red onions and pour the BBQ sauce over the top. Add about 1/4 to 1/2 cup of water to thin out the sauce.
4. Set the slow cooker on low and cook for 8 hours.
5. Once cooked, shred the chicken into the BBQ sauce. Spoon shredded chicken and sauce into the corn tortillas and top with garnishes.
6. Prepare fruit and garnishes.
7. Serve BBQ Chicken Street Tacos with a side of fruit.

Prepare to Freeze Directions

Chop 1 small red onion.

Open, drain and rinse 1 can of black beans.

To a gallon-size plastic freezer baggie, add the following ingredients:
- 4 small boneless, skinless chicken breasts
- 15 oz. can black beans
- Chopped red onion
- 2 cups BBQ sauce

Remove as much air as possible and seal. Add label to baggie and freeze.

Freeze & Thaw Directions

Put the baggie in the freezer and freeze for up to 6 months in a fridge freezer or 12 months in a deep freezer. Thaw in the fridge overnight, or a bowl of lukewarm water for about 20 minutes, before adding the contents of the baggie to the slow cooker with the amount of water listed in the recipe. Set on low and cook for 8 hours. Shred the chicken and make tacos as directed.

Slow Cooker Best Shredded Chicken Tacos

Yield: 4 servings
Prep Time: 10 minutes
Cook Time: 8 hours in slow cooker

Ingredients

- 4 small boneless, skinless chicken breasts
- 3 Tbsp brown sugar
- 1 Tbsp cumin
- 1 Tbsp chili powder
- 1/3 cup red salsa
- 4 oz. can green chiles
- Salt and pepper
- 8 flour tortillas
- Garnish: pico de gallo
- 1 gallon-size freezer baggie

Cooking Directions

1. Add the chicken breasts and add the brown sugar, cumin, chili powder, red salsa and green chilies over the top. Season with a pinch of salt and pepper.
2. Set on low and cook for 8 hours.
3. Once cooked, use 2 forks and shred the chicken into the sauce.
4. Prepare the salad.
5. Serve Slow Cooker Best Shredded Chicken Tacos with pico de gallo garnish and a side salad.

Prepare to Freeze Directions

Open 1 can of green chiles.

To a gallon-size plastic freezer baggie, add the following ingredients:
- 4 small boneless, skinless chicken breasts
- 3 Tbsp brown sugar
- 1 Tbsp cumin
- 1 Tbsp chili powder
- 1/3 cup red salsa
- 4 oz. can green chiles
- Salt and pepper

Remove as much air as possible and seal. Add label to baggie and freeze.

Freeze & Thaw Directions

Put the baggie in the freezer and freeze for up to 6 months in a fridge freezer or 12 months in a deep freezer. Thaw in the fridge overnight, or a bowl of lukewarm water for about 20 minutes, before transferring to the slow cooker and cooking on low for 8 hours. Shred the chicken and make tacos as directed.

Slow Cooker Buffalo Chicken Nachos

Yield:	4 servings
Prep Time:	10 minutes
Cook Time:	8 hours in slow cooker

Ingredients

- 4 small boneless, skinless chicken breasts
- 1 packet ranch dressing mix
- 1 cup buffalo wing sauce
- 1 bag tortilla chips
- 2 cups shredded mozzarella cheese
- Garnish: crumbled blue cheese
- Garnish: chopped celery
- Side: fruit
- 1 gallon-size freezer baggie

Cooking Directions

1. Place the chicken breasts in the base of the slow cooker and sprinkle the ranch dressing mix over the top. Pour the buffalo wing sauce over the top.
2. Set on low and cook for 8 hours.
3. Once the chicken is cooked, shred with 2 forks and combine with the buffalo sauce.
4. Preheat the oven to 400 F.
5. Assemble the nachos on a baking sheet with tortilla chips, shredded buffalo chicken and shredded mozzarella cheese on top. Bake in the preheated oven for 10 to 15 minutes, or until the cheese has melted.
6. Prepare fruit.
7. Serve Buffalo Chicken Nachos with crumbled blue cheese and chopped celery garnish, and side of fruit.

Prepare to Freeze Directions

To a gallon-size plastic freezer baggie, add the following ingredients:
- 4 boneless, skinless chicken breasts
- 1 packet Ranch dressing mix
- 1 cup buffalo wing sauce

Remove as much air as possible and seal. Add label to baggie and freeze.

Freeze & Thaw Directions

Put the baggie in the freezer and freeze for up to 6 months in a fridge freezer or 12 months in a deep freezer. Thaw in the fridge overnight, or a bowl of lukewarm water for about 20 minutes, before transferring to the slow cooker and cooking on low for 8 hours. Shred the chicken, and then assemble the nachos as directed.

Slow Cooker Baja Shredded Chicken Tacos

Yield: 4 servings
Prep Time: 10 minutes
Cook Time: 8 hours in slow cooker

Ingredients

- 4 small boneless, skinless chicken breasts
- 1/4 cup brown sugar
- 1 Tbsp cumin
- 1/3 cup red salsa
- 4 oz. can green chiles
- Salt and pepper
- 8 flour tortillas
- Garnish: pico de gallo
- 1 gallon-size freezer baggie

Cooking Directions

1. Place the chicken breasts into the base of the slow cooker and add the brown sugar, ground cumin, red salsa, green chilies, salt and pepper on top of the chicken.
2. Set the slow cooker on low and cook for 8 hours.
3. Once finished cooking, shred the chicken with 2 forks and mix into the sauce.
4. Spoon the shredded chicken into tortillas and make tacos.
5. Prepare the salad.
6. Serve Slow Cooker Baja Shredded Chicken Tacos with side salad.

Prepare to Freeze Directions

Open 1 can of green chiles.

To a gallon-size plastic freezer baggie, add the following ingredients:
- 4 small boneless, skinless chicken breasts
- 1/4 cup brown sugar
- 1 Tbsp cumin
- 1/3 cup red salsa
- 1 can green chiles
- Salt and pepper

Remove as much air as possible and seal. Add label to baggie and freeze.

Freeze & Thaw Directions

Put the baggie in the freezer and freeze for up to 6 months in a fridge freezer or 12 months in a deep freezer. Thaw in the fridge overnight, or a bowl of lukewarm water for about 20 minutes, before transferring to the slow cooker and cooking on low for 8 hours. Shred the chicken and make tacos as directed.

Slow Cooker Enchilada Chicken

Yield:	4 servings
Prep Time:	10 minutes
Cook Time:	8 hours in slow cooker

Ingredients

- 4 small boneless, skinless chicken breasts
- 12 oz. can enchilada sauce
- 1 cup red salsa
- 1 packet taco seasoning
- Salt and pepper
- 8 flour tortillas
- Garnish: guacamole
- Side: veggies
- 1 gallon-size freezer baggie

Cooking Directions

1. Place the chicken breasts in the slow cooker. Pour the red salsa, red enchilada sauce, and taco seasoning over the top.
2. Set on low and cook for 8 hours.
3. Once finished cooking, shred the chicken into the sauce. Season with salt and pepper to taste.
4. Prepare tacos with the shredded chicken with sauce and guacamole topping.
5. Prepare veggies.
6. Serve Slow Cooker Enchilada Chicken with guacamole and veggies.

Prepare to Freeze Directions

To a gallon-size plastic freezer baggie, add the following ingredients:

- 4 small boneless, skinless chicken breasts
- 12 oz. can red enchilada sauce
- 1 cup red salsa
- 1 packet taco seasoning
- Salt and pepper

Remove as much air as possible and seal. Add label to baggie and freeze.

Freeze & Thaw Directions

Put the baggie in the freezer and freeze for up to 6 months in a fridge freezer or 12 months in a deep freezer. Thaw in the fridge overnight, or a bowl of lukewarm water for about 20 minutes, before adding contents of the bag to the slow cooker. Slow cook as directed. Shred the chicken and make tacos as directed.

Slow Cooker Garlic Parmesan Chicken

Yield:	4 servings
Prep Time:	10 minutes
Cook Time:	8 hours in slow cooker

Ingredients

- 4 small boneless, skinless chicken breasts
- 2 lb. bag baby potatoes
- 3 Tbsp melted butter
- 4 tsp minced garlic
- 1 tsp dried thyme
- Salt and pepper
- Garnish: shredded Parmesan cheese
- Side: veggies
- 1 gallon-size freezer baggie

Cooking Directions

1. Melt the butter and stir in the minced garlic and thyme.
2. Place the chicken breasts and baby potatoes (do not cut) in the base of the slow cooker and pour the melted butter sauce over the top. Add a pinch of salt and pepper.
3. Set on low and cook for 8 hours.
4. Once cooked, spoon the chicken breasts and baby potatoes onto serving bowls and top with shredded Parmesan cheese garnish. Season with salt and pepper to taste.
5. Prepare veggies.
6. Serve Slow Cooker Garlic Parmesan Chicken with shredded Parmesan cheese garnish and side of veggies.

Prepare to Freeze Directions

Melt 3 Tbsp butter and then stir in 4 tsp minced garlic and 1 tsp dried thyme.

To a gallon-size plastic freezer baggie, add the following ingredients:
- 4 boneless, skinless chicken breasts
- 2 lb. bag baby potatoes
- Melted butter sauce

Remove as much air as possible and seal. Add label to baggie and freeze.

Freeze & Thaw Directions

Put the baggie in the freezer and freeze for up to 6 months in a fridge freezer or 12 months in a deep freezer. Thaw in the fridge overnight, or a bowl of lukewarm water for about 20 minutes, before transferring to the slow cooker and cooking on low for 8 hours.

Slow Cooker Margarita Chicken

Yield:	4 servings
Prep Time:	10 minutes
Cook Time:	8 hours in slow cooker

Ingredients

- 4 small boneless, skinless chicken breasts
- 1 cup limeade
- 1/2 cup orange juice
- 4 tsp minced garlic
- 1/4 tsp cayenne pepper
- Salt and pepper
- Garnish: chopped cilantro
- Side: rice
- Side: veggies
- 1 gallon-size freezer baggie

Cooking Directions

1. In a small mixing bowl, whisk together the limeade, orange juice, minced garlic, cayenne pepper and a few pinches of salt and pepper.
2. Place the chicken breasts in the base of the slow cooker and pour the marinade over the top.
3. Set on low and cook for 8 hours.
4. Once cooked, remove from the sauce and slice or shred the chicken.
5. Cook the rice, as directed.
6. Prepare veggies.
7. Serve Slow Cooker Margarita Chicken with chopped cilantro garnish over rice with veggies.

Prepare to Freeze Directions

To a gallon-size plastic freezer baggie, add the following ingredients:
- 4 small boneless, skinless chicken breasts
- 1 cup limeade
- 1/2 cup orange juice
- 4 tsp minced garlic
- 1/4 tsp cayenne pepper
- Salt and pepper

Remove as much air as possible and seal. Add label to baggie and freeze.

Freeze & Thaw Directions

Put the baggie in the freezer and freeze for up to 6 months in a fridge freezer or 12 months in a deep freezer. Thaw in the fridge overnight, or a bowl of lukewarm water for about 20 minutes, before transferring to the slow cooker and cooking on low for 8 hours.

Slow Cooker Pepperoni Chicken

Yield: 4 servings
Prep Time: 10 minutes
Cook Time: 6 hours in slow cooker

Ingredients

- 4 small boneless, skinless chicken breasts
- 1 1/2 cups pizza sauce
- 20 pepperonis
- 1 cup shredded mozzarella cheese
- Salt and pepper
- Garnish: grated Parmesan cheese
- Side: pasta
- Side: veggies
- 1 gallon-size freezer baggie

Cooking Directions

1. Place the chicken breasts in the base of the slow cooker and pour the pizza sauce directly over the chicken. Add the pepperonis around and on top of the chicken.
2. Set on low and cook for 6 hours.
3. With 30 minutes remaining in the cooking cycle, add the shredded mozzarella cheese right onto each piece of chicken and let finish cooking. Use a slotted spoon to remove the chicken and drain the juices from the slow cooker. Garnish with grated Parmesan cheese.
4. Cook the pasta as directed.
5. Prepare veggies.
6. Serve Slow Cooker Pepperoni Chicken over pasta rice with veggies.

Freeze & Thaw Directions

To a gallon-size plastic freezer baggie, add the following ingredients:
- 4 small boneless, skinless chicken breasts
- 1 1/2 cups pizza sauce
- 20 pepperonis

Remove as much air as possible and seal. Add label to baggie and freeze.

Prepare to Freeze Directions

Put the baggie in the freezer and freeze for up to 6 months in a fridge freezer or 12 months in a deep freezer. Thaw in the fridge overnight, or a bowl of lukewarm water for about 20 minutes, before transferring to the slow cooker and cooking on low for 6 hours.

If slow cooking from frozen or partially frozen, add ½ cup of water or chicken stock to the slow cooker insert and change the slow cook time to low for 8 hours.

Slow Cooker Ranch Chicken Tacos

Yield: 4 servings
Prep Time: 10 minutes
Cook Time: 8 hours in slow cooker

Ingredients

- 4 small boneless, skinless chicken breasts
- 1/2 cup chicken stock
- 1 packet ranch dressing mix
- 1 packet taco seasoning
- Salt and pepper
- 8 flour tortillas
- Garnish: coleslaw
- Garnish: Ranch salad dressing
- Side: salad
- 1 gallon-size freezer baggie

Cooking Directions

1. Place the chicken breasts in the base of the slow cooker. Season with salt and pepper.
2. In a small mixing bowl, whisk the chicken stock and Ranch dressing mix together and pour over the chicken. Sprinkle the taco seasoning on top.
3. Set on low and cook for 8 hours.
4. Once cooked, strain off excess liquid and shred the chicken into the sauce. Season with salt and pepper as needed. Assemble tacos with shredded chicken, coleslaw and Ranch dressing into tortillas.
5. Prepare the salad.
6. Serve Slow Cooker Ranch Chicken Tacos with coleslaw garnish and side salad.

Prepare to Freeze Directions

To a gallon-size plastic freezer baggie, add the following ingredients:
- 4 boneless, skinless chicken breasts
- 1/2 cup chicken stock
- 1 packet Ranch dressing mix
- 1 packet taco seasoning
- Salt and pepper

Remove as much air as possible and seal. Add label to baggie and freeze.

Freeze & Thaw Directions

Put the baggie in the freezer and freeze for up to 6 months in a fridge freezer or 12 months in a deep freezer. Thaw in the fridge overnight, or a bowl of lukewarm water for about 20 minutes, before transferring to the slow cooker and cooking on low for 8 hours. Shred the chicken and make tacos as directed.

Slow Cooker Ranchero Chicken

Yield: 4 servings
Prep Time: 10 minutes
Cook Time: 8 hours in slow cooker

Ingredients

- 15 oz. can diced tomatoes
- 6 oz. can tomato paste
- 3 Tbsp taco seasoning
- 2 small boneless, skinless chicken breasts
- 4 boneless, skinless chicken thighs
- Salt and pepper
- Side: rice
- Side: veggies
- 1 gallon-size freezer baggie

Cooking Directions

1. Whisk together the diced tomatoes with their juices and the tomato paste in the base of the slow cooker. Stir in the taco seasoning.
2. Add the chicken breast and thighs to sauce and spoon the sauce over the top.
3. Set the slow cooker on low and cook for 8 hours.
4. Once cooked, pull apart the chicken with 2 forks.
5. Cook rice, as directed.
6. Prepare veggies.
7. Serve Ranchero Chicken over rice with a side of veggies.

Prepare to Freeze Directions

Open 1 can of diced tomatoes. Open 1 can of tomato paste.

To a gallon-size plastic freezer baggie, add the following ingredients:
- 15 oz. can diced tomatoes
- 6 oz. can tomato paste
- 3 Tbsp taco seasoning
- 2 small boneless, skinless chicken breasts
- 4 boneless, skinless chicken thighs
- Salt and pepper

Remove as much air as possible and seal. Add label to baggie and freeze.

Freeze & Thaw Directions

Put the baggie in the freezer and freeze for up to 6 months in a fridge freezer or 12 months in a deep freezer. Thaw in the fridge overnight, or a bowl of lukewarm water for about 20 minutes, before transferring to the slow cooker and cooking on low for 8 hours. Shred the chicken and serve as directed.

Slow Cooker Shredded Hawaiian Chicken Sandwiches

Yield: 4 servings
Prep Time: 10 minutes
Cook Time: 8 hours on low

Ingredients

- 4 small boneless, skinless chicken breasts
- Salt and pepper
- 1/4 cup BBQ sauce
- 8 oz. can crushed pineapple
- 1 small red onion
- 4 hamburger buns
- Side: chips
- Side: fruit
- 1 gallon-size freezer baggie

Cooking Directions

1. Place the chicken breasts into the base of the slow cooker. Sprinkle a little salt and pepper over the top. Drizzle BBQ sauce over the chicken breasts and then pour the pineapple juices around the chicken breasts and the crushed pineapple on top of the chicken.
2. Note: I like to add the onions raw after the chicken has cooked, but if you'd like to add them in while it all cooks, you can drop them in with the crushed pineapple.
3. Set on low and cook for 8 hours.
4. Once cooked, pull out the chicken breasts and the pineapple and add to a bowl, then shred with 2 forks. Mix in the chopped red onion, if you didn't add it to the slow cooker.
5. Prepare fruit, as needed.
6. Serve Slow Cooker Shredded Hawaiian Chicken Sandwiches with fruit and chips.

Prepare to Freeze Directions

Finely chop 1 small red onion.

Open 1 can of crushed pineapple. Do not drain.

To a gallon-size plastic freezer baggie, add the following ingredients:
- 4 small boneless, skinless chicken breasts
- Salt and pepper
- 1/4 cup BBQ sauce
- 8 oz. can pineapple, undrained
- Finely chopped onion

Remove as much air as possible and seal. Add label to baggie and freeze.

Freeze & Thaw Directions

Put the baggie in the freezer and freeze for up to 6 months in a fridge freezer or 12 months in a deep freezer. Thaw in the fridge overnight, or a bowl of lukewarm water for about 20 minutes, before transferring to the slow cooker and cooking on low for 8 hours. Shred the chicken, and assemble sandwiches as directed.

Slow Cooker Thai Peanut Chicken

Yield: 4 servings
Prep Time: 10 minutes
Cook Time: 8 hours in slow cooker

Ingredients

- 4 small boneless, skinless chicken breasts
- Salt and pepper
- 1 small white onion
- 1 red bell pepper
- 2 cups Thai peanut sauce
- 1 Tbsp cornstarch
- Garnish: sesame seeds
- Garnish: chopped peanuts
- Side: rice
- Side: veggies
- 1 gallon-size freezer baggie

Cooking Directions

1. Cut up the chicken into 1/2 inch pieces.
2. Dice the onion and red bell pepper into 1-inch pieces.
3. Place the chicken pieces in the base of the slow cooker and add the diced onion and red bell pepper around the chicken. Season with salt and pepper. Pour the Thai peanut sauce over the top.
4. Set on low and cook for 8 hours.
5. With 30 minutes left in the cooking cycle, swirl the cornstarch with 2 Tbsp of water and stir it into the sauce in the slow cooker. Slow cook for 30 more minutes to allow sauce to thicken.
6. Cook the rice as directed.
7. Prepare veggies.
8. Serve Slow Cooker Thai Peanut Chicken with chopped peanuts and sesame seeds garnish, over rice with veggies.

Prepare to Freeze Directions

Cut up 4 chicken breasts into 1/2-inch pieces.

Dice 1 small onion and 1 red bell pepper into 1-inch pieces.

To a gallon-size plastic freezer baggie, add the following ingredients:
- Chicken pieces
- Diced onion
- Diced red bell peppers
- 2 cups Thai peanut sauce
- Do NOT add the cornstarch before freezing.

Remove as much air as possible and seal. Add label to baggie and freeze.

Freeze & Thaw Directions

Put the baggie in the freezer and freeze for up to 6 months in a fridge freezer or 12 months in a deep freezer. Thaw in the fridge overnight, or a bowl of lukewarm water for about 20 minutes, before transferring to the slow cooker and cooking on low for 8 hours. Thicken with cornstarch slurry at the end of the cooking cycle as directed.

Sweet Potato Chicken Sausage Hash

Yield: 4 servings
Prep Time: 10 minutes
Cook Time: 20 minutes

Ingredients

- 2 Tbsp olive oil
- 2 large sweet potatoes
- 1 red bell pepper
- 1 green bell pepper
- 2 Tbsp minced onion
- 1 tsp garlic powder
- 1 tsp ground ginger
- Salt and pepper
- 5 pre-cooked chicken sausage links
- 1 gallon-size freezer baggie

Cooking Directions

1. Peel and cube the sweet potatoes into ½-inch size pieces.
2. Seed and chop the red and green bell peppers.
3. Slice the chicken sausage links into ½-inch slices.
4. To a large skillet with a tight fitting lid, add the olive oil and saute the sweet potato cubes for 5 to 7 minutes, adding water if needed to help them 'steam' and from sticking to the bottom. Stir often.
5. Stir in the diced green and red bell peppers, minced onion, garlic powder, ground ginger and salt and pepper. Saute for another 5 minutes, or until peppers have softened.
6. Add in the chicken sausage slices and stir into the veggies. Saute together for a few minutes, or until the sweet potatoes are all completely tender and chicken sausage is warmed.
7. Note: If you are using raw sausage links, make sure it has time to cook through, or cook them in a separate skillet before mixing all together.
8. Serve Sweet Potato & Chicken Sausage Skillet Dinner.

Prepare to Freeze Directions

Slice the 5 chicken sausage links.

Dice the 1 red and 1 green bell pepper.

Peel 2 large sweet potatoes and cut into 1-inch cubes.

To a gallon-size plastic freezer baggie, add the following ingredients:
- 2 Tbsp olive oil
- Diced sweet potatoes
- Chopped red and green bell peppers
- Sliced chicken sausage
- 2 Tbsp minced onion
- 1 tsp garlic powder
- 1 tsp ground ginger
- Salt and pepper

Remove as much air as possible and seal. Add label to baggie and freeze.

Freeze & Thaw Directions

Put the baggie in the freezer and freeze for up to 6 months in a fridge freezer or 12 months in a deep freezer. Thaw in the fridge overnight, or a bowl of lukewarm water for about 20 minutes. Add the contents of the freezer baggie to the skillet with about 3/4 cup warm water. Bring to bubbling over medium high heat and then cover and reduce heat to low and simmer for 20 minutes, or until sweet potatoes are tender and sausage is warmed. Stir often.

Chapter 2 – 5-Ingredient Beef Recipes

Baked Apricot Meatballs

Baked Chunky Marinara Ravioli

Baked Marinara Meatballs

Grilled Campfire Burgers

Grilled Cheddar Bacon Burgers

Grilled Ranch Burgers

Grilled Teriyaki Burgers

Instant Pot One Pot Spaghetti

Slow Cooker 3-Packet Pot Roast

Slow Cooker Mississippi Beef Roast

Slow Cooker Russian Shredded Beef Sandwiches

Slow Cooker Sloppy Shredded Beef Sandwiches

Slow Cooker Santa Fe Beef

Skillet Cheesy Hamburger Helper

Skillet Nacho Dip

Skillet Sloppy Joes

Stovetop 5-Ingredient Chili

Stovetop Classic Spaghetti Sauce

Baked Apricot Meatballs

Yield: 4 servings
Prep Time: 10 minutes
Cook Time: 35 minutes

Ingredients

- 24 frozen pre-cooked meatballs
- 1 cup apricot preserves
- 1/2 cup French salad dressing
- Side: rice
- Side: salad
- 9x13-inch disposable foil tray

Cooking Directions

1. Preheat the oven to 375 F.
2. Spread the frozen meatballs into the base of a 9x13-inch baking dish.
3. In a small mixing bowl, combine the apricot preserves and French salad dressing. Pour over the meatballs in the baking dish, coating each one. Cover with foil.
4. Bake in the preheated oven for 30 to 35 minutes, or until cooked through.
5. Cook the rice, as directed.
6. Prepare the salad.
7. Serve Apricot Meatballs over rice with salad.

Prepare to Freeze Directions

In a small mixing bowl, combine 1 cup apricot preserves and 1/2 cup French salad dressing.

To the disposable tray, add the following ingredients:
- Pre-cooked meatballs
- Prepared apricot sauce, coating the meatballs

Cover with foil or lid, add label and freeze.

Freeze & Thaw Directions

Put the tray in the freezer and freeze for up to 6 months in a fridge freezer or 12 months in a deep freezer. Thaw in the fridge overnight, before transferring to the oven and baking with foil cover, as directed.

Baked Chunky Marinara Ravioli

Yield:	4 servings
Prep Time:	10 minutes
Cook Time:	25 minutes

Ingredients

- 20 oz. fresh or frozen ravioli
- 26 oz. jar chunky marinara
- Salt and pepper
- 1/2 cup Parmesan cheese
- 1 1/2 cups shredded mozzarella cheese
- Garnish: fresh basil
- Side: veggies
- Side: salad
- 9x13-inch disposable foil tray

Cooking Directions

1. Preheat the oven to 350 F. Lightly spray a 9x13-inch baking dish with non-stick cooking spray.
2. Place the ravioli into the base of the baking dish and pour 1 cup of hot water over the top. Then pour the chunky marinara sauce over the top and then sprinkle with salt and pepper.
3. Sprinkle the grated Parmesan cheese on top and then the shredded mozzarella cheese over the top.
4. Bake in the preheated oven for 25 minutes, or until ravioli in the middle is softened and the cheese on top is golden brown.
5. Chop the basil for the garnish.
6. Prepare the veggies and salad.
7. Serve Baked Chunky Marinara Ravioli with fresh basil garnish, veggies and salad.

Prepare to Freeze Directions

To the disposable tray, layer the following ingredients:
- 20 oz. package fresh or frozen ravioli
- 26 oz. jar chunky marinara sauce
- Salt and pepper
- 1/2 cup grated Parmesan cheese
- 1 1/2 cups shredded mozzarella cheese
- Do NOT add hot water to the freezer tray.

Cover with foil or lid, add label to top and freeze.

Freeze & Thaw Directions

Put the tray in the freezer and freeze for up to 6 months in a fridge freezer or 12 months in a deep freezer. Thaw in the fridge overnight, or a bowl of lukewarm water for about 20 minutes, before adding the HOT water around the edges of the tray, and baking as directed.

Baked Marinara Meatballs

Yield: 4 servings
Prep Time: 10 minutes
Cook Time: 35 minutes

Ingredients

- 1 1/2 lbs. lean ground beef
- 1 egg
- 1/2 cup Italian seasoned breadcrumbs
- 2 cups chunky marinara sauce
- Side: pasta
- Side: salad
- 9x13-inch disposable foil tray

Cooking Directions

1. Preheat the oven to 350 F.
2. In a large mixing bowl, combine the lean ground beef, eggs and breadcrumbs and form into about 18 small meatballs. Add the meatballs to a 9x13-inch baking dish. Pour the chunky marinara sauce directly over the meatballs.
3. Bake in the preheated oven for 30 to 35 minutes, or until cooked through. Cooking time may vary depending on the size of the meatballs.
4. Cook the pasta, as directed.
5. Prepare the salad.
6. Serve Baked Marinara Meatballs over pasta with salad.

Prepare to Freeze Directions

In a large mixing bowl, combine 1 1/2 lbs. lean ground beef, 1 egg, 1/2 cup Italian seasoned breadcrumbs. Form about 18 small meatballs and place them in a single layer into the disposable baking dish.

To the disposable tray, add the following ingredients:
- Pre-made meatballs
- 2 cups chunky marinara sauce directly onto the meatballs

Cover with foil or lid, add label and freeze.

Freeze & Thaw Directions

Put the tray in the freezer and freeze for up to 6 months in a fridge freezer or 12 months in a deep freezer. Thaw in the fridge overnight, or a tray/pan of warm water for about 20 minutes, before transferring to the oven and baking as directed.

If baking from frozen or partially frozen, keep the dish covered tightly with foil and double the baking time. Bake until meat is cooked through.

Grilled Campfire Burgers

Yield: 4 servings
Prep Time: 10 minutes
Cook Time: 12 minutes

Ingredients

- 1 lb. ground beef
- 1 tsp minced garlic
- 1 tsp Worcestershire sauce
- 1 tsp salt
- 1/2 cup BBQ sauce
- 2 Tbsp mayonnaise
- 4 slices cheddar cheese
- 4 hamburger buns
- Side: chips
- Side: fruit
- 1 gallon-size freezer baggie

Cooking Directions

1. Preheat the grill.
2. Combine the ground beef, minced garlic, Worcestershire sauce and salt. Form into 4 patties.
3. Place the patties on the grill. Grill for 5 to 6 minutes per side, or until internal temperature should reach 165 F. If you need to cook the patties a little longer then you can move them to a cool part of the grill until they're done.
4. Meanwhile, stir together the BBQ and mayonnaise.
5. Once burgers are cooked, assemble with cheddar cheese and BBQ-mayo sauce on buns.
6. Serve Campfire Burgers with fruit and/or chips.

Prepare to Freeze Directions

Combine 1 lb. ground beef with 1 tsp minced garlic, 1 tsp Worcestershire sauce, and 1 tsp salt in a medium mixing bowl. Form into 4 patties.

To a gallon-size plastic freezer baggie, add the following ingredients:
- 4 burger patties
- Foil or parchment paper between patties to keep from sticking together

Remove as much air as possible and seal. Add label to baggie and freeze.

Freeze & Thaw Directions

Put the baggie in the freezer and freeze for up to 6 months in a fridge freezer or 12 months in a deep freezer. Thaw completely in the fridge before grilling the burgers. Make sauce and assemble burgers, as directed.

Grilled Cheddar Bacon Burgers

Yield: 4 servings
Prep Time: 10 minutes
Cook Time: 12 minutes

Ingredients

- 1 lb. ground beef
- 1/2 cup bacon crumbles
- 1 tsp minced garlic
- 1 tsp salt
- 4 hamburger buns
- 4 slices sharp cheddar cheese
- 4 Tbsp BBQ sauce
- Side: chips
- Side: fruit
- 1 gallon-size freezer baggie

Cooking Directions

1. Preheat the grill.
2. Combine the ground beef, bacon crumbles, minced garlic and salt in a medium mixing bowl. Form into 4 patties.
3. Place the patties on the grill. Grill for 5 to 6 minutes per side, or until internal temperature should reach 165 F. If you need to cook the patties a little longer then you can move them to a cool part of the grill until they're cooked to your liking.
4. Once cooked, top with sliced sharp cheddar cheese and BBQ sauce.
5. Serve Cheddar Bacon Burgers with fruit and chips.

Prepare to Freeze Directions

Combine 1 lb. ground beef, 1/2 cup bacon crumbles, 1 tsp minced garlic, and 1 tsp salt in a medium mixing bowl. Form into 4 patties.

To a gallon-size plastic freezer baggie, add the following ingredients:
- 4 burger patties
- Foil or parchment paper between patties to keep from sticking together

Remove as much air as possible and seal. Add label to baggie and freeze.

Freeze & Thaw Directions

Put the baggie in the freezer and freeze for up to 6 months in a fridge freezer or 12 months in a deep freezer. Thaw completely in the fridge before grilling the burgers. Assemble burgers with toppings as directed.

Grilled Ranch Burgers

Yield: 4 servings
Prep Time: 10 minutes
Cook Time: 12 minutes

Ingredients

- 1 lb. ground beef
- 1 Tbsp dry Ranch salad dressing mix
- Salt and pepper
- 4 hamburger buns
- 1/2 cup Ranch salad dressing
- Side: fruit
- Side: chips
- 1 gallon-size freezer baggie

Cooking Directions

1. Mix the ground beef and Ranch dressing mix together. Make 4 burger patties and season both sides with salt and pepper.
2. Place the patties on the grill. Grill for 5 to 6 minutes per side, or until internal temperature should reach 165 F. If you need to cook the patties a little longer then you can move them to a cool part of the grill until they're cooked to your liking.
3. Once cooked, top with Ranch salad dressing.
4. Serve Grilled Ranch Burgers with fruit and chips.

Prepare to Freeze Directions

Mix 1 lb. ground beef, and 1 Tbsp dry Ranch dressing mix together. Form 4 burger patties.

To a gallon-size plastic freezer baggie, add the following ingredients:
- 4 burger patties
- Foil or parchment paper between patties to keep from sticking together

Remove as much air as possible and seal. Add label to baggie and freeze.

Freeze & Thaw Directions

Put the baggie in the freezer and freeze for up to 6 months in a fridge freezer or 12 months in a deep freezer. Thaw completely in the fridge before grilling the burgers. Assemble burgers as directed.

Grilled Teriyaki Burgers

Yield: 4 servings
Prep Time: 10 minutes
Cook Time: 12 minutes

Ingredients

- 1 1/2 lbs. ground beef
- 1/4 cup mayonnaise
- 3 Tbsp teriyaki sauce
- Salt and pepper
- 8 oz. can pineapple slices
- 4 hamburger buns
- Garnish: teriyaki sauce
- Garnish: lettuce leaves
- Side: chips
- Side: fruit
- 1 gallon-size freezer baggie

Cooking Directions

1. In a small bowl, whisk together the mayonnaise and teriyaki sauce.
2. In a large bowl, mix ground beef and the mayo-teriyaki combo. Make 4 burger patties and season both sides with salt and pepper.
3. Preheat the grill. Pull out 4 pineapple slices and pat dry.
4. Place the patties on the grill. Grill for 5 to 6 minutes per side, or until internal temperature should reach 165 F. If you need to cook the patties a little longer then you can move them to a cool part of the grill until they're cooked to your liking.
5. Grill the dried pineapple slices for 1 minute on each side. Set patties onto buns with grilled pineapple slice, and top with dollop of teriyaki sauce. Add lettuce leaves to the burger.
6. Serve Grilled Teriyaki Burgers with fruit and chips.

Prepare to Freeze Directions

Mix together 1/4 cup mayonnaise with 3 Tbsp teriyaki sauce.

Mix 1 1/2 lbs. ground beef with the mayo-teriyaki combo. Form 4 burger patties.

To a gallon-size plastic freezer baggie, add the following ingredients:
- Burger patties
- Foil or parchment paper between patties to keep from sticking together
- Do NOT freeze the pineapple slices. Leave those in your pantry until cook day.

Remove as much air as possible and seal. Add label to baggie and freeze.

Freeze & Thaw Directions

Put the baggie in the freezer and freeze for up to 6 months in a fridge freezer or 12 months in a deep freezer. Thaw completely in the fridge before grilling the burgers and pineapple slices. Assemble burgers as directed.

Instant Pot One Pot Spaghetti

Yield: 4 servings
Prep Time: 15 minutes
Cook Time: 6 minutes plus pressure build and release time

Ingredients

- 1 lb. lean ground beef
- 1 Tbsp minced onion
- 1 tsp garlic powder
- 26 oz. jar marinara sauce
- 16 oz. spaghetti noodles
- 2 1/2 cups beef stock
- Garnish: Parmesan cheese
- Side: salad
- 1 gallon-size freezer baggie

Cooking Directions

1. Add the lean ground beef, minced onion, and garlic powder to the electric pressure cooker insert. Set on Saute mode and brown the ground beef in the insert for 5 to 6 minutes. Once browned, stir in the marinara sauce.
2. Break the noodles in half or thirds and mix into the sauce and then pour the beef stock over the top. Give it a gentle stir and then press all the noodles into the liquid.
3. Close the lid, set to sealing.
4. Set on Manual, High Pressure and cook for 6 minutes.
5. Let naturally release for 5 minutes, then finish the release by setting to Venting.
6. The sauce will look too thin, but give it a stir and it will thicken up with the pasta and meat.
7. Serve Instant Pot One-Pot Spaghetti with Parmesan cheese garnish, and a side salad.

Prepare to Freeze Directions

Brown 1 lb. lean ground beef with 1 Tbsp minced onion and 1 tsp garlic powder, in a skillet.

To a gallon-size plastic freezer baggie in a round bowl/dish, add the following ingredients:
- Ground beef, browned and cooled
- 26 oz. jar marinara sauce
- Salt and pepper
- Do NOT add beef stock or pasta to the freezer meal bag, add that at time of pressure cooking.

Remove as much air as possible and seal. Add label to baggie and freeze.

Freeze & Thaw Directions

Put the baggie in the freezer and freeze for up to 6 months in a fridge freezer or 12 months in a deep freezer. Thaw completely. Transfer to pressure cooker, then pressure cook as directed with broken pasta and 2 1/2 cups beef stock, chicken stock or water.

Slow Cooker 3-Packet Pot Roast

Yield: 4 servings
Prep Time: 10 minutes
Cook Time: 8 hours in slow cooker

Ingredients

- 2 lb. beef chuck roast
- 2 lb. bag baby potatoes
- Salt and pepper
- 1 packet Italian dressing mix
- 1 packet Ranch dressing mix
- 1 packet gravy mix
- 1 cup water
- Side: salad
- 1 gallon-size freezer baggie

Cooking Directions

1. Place the beef roast and baby potatoes into the base of the slow cooker and season with salt and pepper.
2. In a small mixing bowl, whisk together the 3 packets of dry mix and the water. Pour directly onto the beef roast. If your slow cooker "runs hot" and dries out meat, pour an additional 1/2 cup of water into the base of the slow cooker.
3. Set the slow cooker on low and cook for 8 hours.
4. Once finished cooking, slice or shred the beef with 2 forks and mix into the sauce.
5. Prepare salad.
6. Serve Slow Cooker 3-Packet Pot Roast with baby potatoes and side salad.

Prepare to Freeze Directions

In a small mixing bowl, whisk together 1 packet of Italian dressing mix, 1 packet of Ranch dressing mix, 1 packet of gravy mix with 1 cup of water.

To a gallon-size plastic freezer baggie, add the following ingredients:
- 2 lb. beef chuck roast
- 2 lb. bag baby potatoes
- Salt and pepper
- Prepared sauce

Remove as much air as possible and seal. Add label to baggie and freeze.

Freeze & Thaw Directions

Put the baggie in the freezer and freeze for up to 6 months in a fridge freezer or 12 months in a deep freezer. Thaw in the fridge overnight, or a bowl of lukewarm water for about 20 minutes, before transferring to the slow cooker and cooking on low for 8 hours.

Slow Cooker Mississippi Beef Roast

Yield: 4 servings
Prep Time: 10 minutes
Cook Time: 8 hours in slow cooker

Ingredients

- 2 lb. beef chuck roast
- 1 packet Ranch dressing mix
- 8 pepperoncini peppers
- 2 Tbsp butter
- 1 tsp pepper
- Side: dinner rolls
- Side: veggies
- 1 gallon-size freezer baggie

Cooking Directions

1. Slice the butter into 2-3 pieces.
2. Place the beef roast in the base of the slow cooker and season with Ranch dressing mix. Add the pepperoncini peppers, butter slices directly on the roast and sprinkle the pepper over the top.
3. Set the slow cooker on low and cook for 8 hours.
4. Warm the dinner rolls.
5. Prepare veggies.
6. Serve Slow Cooker Mississippi Beef Roast with veggies and dinner rolls.

Prepare to Freeze Directions

Slice 2 Tbsp butter into 2-3 pieces.

To a gallon-size plastic freezer baggie, add the following ingredients:
- 2 lb. beef chuck roast
- 1 packet Ranch dressing mix
- 8 pepperoncini peppers
- Butter slices
- 1 tsp pepper

Remove as much air as possible and seal. Add label to baggie and freeze.

Freeze & Thaw Directions

Put the baggie in the freezer and freeze for up to 6 months in a fridge freezer or 12 months in a deep freezer. Thaw in the fridge overnight, or a bowl of lukewarm water for about 20 minutes, before transferring to the slow cooker and cooking on low for 8 hours.

Slow Cooker Russian Shredded Beef Sandwiches

Yield: 4 servings
Prep Time: 10 minutes
Cook Time: 8 hours in slow cooker

Ingredients

- 2 lb. beef chuck roast
- Salt and pepper
- 1 cup Russian salad dressing
- 1 Tbsp minced onion
- 1 tsp garlic powder
- Salt and pepper
- 4 hoagie rolls
- Garnish: coleslaw
- Side: fruit
- 1 gallon-size freezer baggie

Cooking Directions

1. Place the beef roast into the base of the slow cooker and season with salt and pepper. Pour the Russian salad dressing over the top and sprinkle the minced onion and garlic powder over the top.
2. Set the slow cooker on low and cook for 8 hours.
3. Once finished cooking, shred the beef with 2 forks and mix into the sauce.
4. Prepare the Coleslaw, and assemble sandwiches with shredded beef and Coleslaw.
5. Prepare the fruit.
6. Serve Russian Shredded Beef Sandwiches with a side of fruit.

Prepare to Freeze Directions

To a gallon-size plastic freezer baggie, add the following ingredients:

- 2 lb. beef chuck roast
- Salt and pepper
- 1 cup Russian salad dressing
- 1 Tbsp minced onion
- 1 tsp garlic powder

Remove as much air as possible and seal. Add label to baggie and freeze.

Freeze & Thaw Directions

Put the baggie in the freezer and freeze for up to 6 months in a fridge freezer or 12 months in a deep freezer. Thaw in the fridge overnight, or a bowl of lukewarm water for about 20 minutes, before transferring to the slow cooker and cooking on low for 8 hours. Shred the beef and prepare sandwiches as directed.

Slow Cooker Sloppy Shredded Beef Sandwiches

Yield: 4 servings
Prep Time: 10 minutes
Cook Time: 8 hours in slow cooker

Ingredients

- 2 lb. beef chuck roast
- Salt and pepper
- 1 small white onion
- 15 oz. can diced tomatoes
- 15 oz. can sloppy joe sauce
- 4 hamburger buns
- Side: salad
- Side: fruit
- 1 gallon-size freezer baggie

Cooking Directions

1. Slice the onion into half moons.
2. Open and drain the diced tomatoes. Open the sloppy joe sauce.
3. Place the beef roast into the base of the slow cooker and season with salt and pepper. Sprinkle the sliced onions over the top, then pour the diced tomatoes and sloppy joe sauce over the top.
4. Set the slow cooker on low and cook for 8 hours.
5. Once finished cooking, shred the beef with 2 forks and mix into the sauce. Assemble sandwiches with hamburger buns and meat sauce.
6. Prepare salad and fruit.
7. Serve Sloppy Shredded Beef Sandwiches with salad and fruit.

Prepare to Freeze Directions

Slice 1 white onion into half moons.

Open and drain 1 can of diced tomatoes. Open 1 can of sloppy joe sauce.

To a gallon-size plastic freezer baggie, add the following ingredients:
- 2 lb. beef chuck roast
- Salt and pepper
- Sliced onions
- Drained diced tomatoes
- Sloppy joe sauce

Remove as much air as possible and seal. Add label to baggie and freeze.

Freeze & Thaw Directions

Put the baggie in the freezer and freeze for up to 6 months in a fridge freezer or 12 months in a deep freezer. Thaw in the fridge overnight, or a bowl of lukewarm water for about 20 minutes, before transferring to the slow cooker and cooking on low for 8 hours. Shred the beef with the sauce, and assemble sandwiches as directed.

Slow Cooker Santa Fe Beef

Yield: 4 servings
Prep Time: 10 minutes
Cook Time: 8 hours in slow cooker

Ingredients

- 2 lb. beef chuck roast
- Salt and pepper
- 1 packet taco seasoning
- 4 oz. can green chiles
- 1 cup red salsa
- Side: salad
- Side: dinner rolls
- 1 gallon-size freezer baggie

Cooking Directions

1. Place the beef roast into the base of the slow cooker and season with salt and pepper. Sprinkle the taco seasoning over the roast. Pour the green chilies and red salsa over the top.
2. Set the slow cooker on low and cook for 8 hours.
3. Once finished cooking, shred the beef with 2 forks and mix into the sauce.
4. Prepare salad.
5. Warm the dinner rolls.
6. Serve Slow Cooker Santa Fe Beef with salad and dinner rolls.

Prepare to Freeze Directions

Open 1 can of green chiles.

To a gallon-size plastic freezer baggie, add the following ingredients:
- 2 lb. beef chuck roast
- Salt and pepper
- 1 packet taco seasoning
- 4 oz. can green chilies
- 1 cup red salsa

Remove as much air as possible and seal. Add label to baggie and freeze.

Freeze & Thaw Directions

Put the baggie in the freezer and freeze for up to 6 months in a fridge freezer or 12 months in a deep freezer. Thaw in the fridge overnight, or a bowl of lukewarm water for about 20 minutes, before transferring to the slow cooker and cooking on low for 8 hours. Shred the beef before serving.

Skillet Cheesy Hamburger Helper

Yield: 4 servings
Prep Time: 15 minutes
Cook Time: 20 minutes

Ingredients

- 1 lb. ground beef
- 1 Tbsp minced onion
- 1 tsp garlic powder
- 15 oz. can tomato sauce
- 1 Tbsp Italian seasoning
- 12 oz. pasta
- 2 cups beef stock
- Salt and pepper
- Topping: 2 cups shredded mild cheddar cheese
- Side: veggies
- 1 gallon-size freezer baggie

Cooking Directions

1. Open the cans of tomato sauce.
2. In a large skillet, brown the ground beef with the minced onion and garlic powder. Drain and return to the skillet. Stir in the tomato sauce and Italian seasoning, and bring to bubbling. Then pour in the pasta and the beef stock. Press the pasta into the beef stock, cover and simmer over medium low heat for 10 minutes, or until pasta is softened.
3. Remove from heat immediately to keep pasta from overcooking. Season with salt and pepper to taste. Sprinkle shredded cheese over the beef-pasta mixture.
4. Prepare veggies.
5. Serve Cheesy Hamburger Helper with veggies.

Prepare to Freeze Directions

Brown 1 lb. ground beef with 1 Tbsp minced onion and 1 tsp garlic powder. Let cool.

Open 1 can of tomato sauce.

To a gallon-size plastic freezer baggie, add the following ingredients:
- Browned, cooled ground beef
- 15 oz. can tomato sauce
- Salt and pepper
- 1 Tbsp Italian seasoning
- Do NOT freeze pasta, beef stock or shredded cheese with other ingredients.

Remove as much air as possible and seal. Add label to baggie and freeze.

Freeze & Thaw Directions

Put the baggie in the freezer and freeze for up to 6 months in a fridge freezer or 12 months in a deep freezer. Thaw in the fridge overnight, or a bowl of lukewarm water for about 20 minutes, before transferring to a large skillet and reheating. Once bubbling, add the pasta and beef stock, cover and simmer for 10 minutes, or until pasta is cooked. Top with shredded cheese before serving.

Skillet Nacho Dip

Yield:	4 servings
Prep Time:	10 minutes
Cook Time:	20 minutes

Ingredients

- 1 lb. ground beef
- 2 Tbsp minced onion
- 1 tsp garlic powder
- 15 oz. can pinto beans
- 10 oz. can diced tomatoes & green chiles
- 1 packet taco seasoning
- 2 cups shredded cheddar cheese
- 1 bag tortilla chips
- Garnish: chopped red bell pepper
- Garnish: diced avocado
- Side: salad
- 1 gallon-size freezer baggie

Cooking Directions

1. Open, drain and rinse the pinto beans. Open the diced tomatoes with green chiles.
2. In a large skillet, brown the ground beef with the minced onion and garlic powder. Drain and return to the skillet. Stir in the rinsed pinto beans, diced tomatoes with green chilies, and taco seasoning. Combine well and bring to bubbling over medium low heat.
3. Just before serving, sprinkle the shredded cheddar cheese over the top and let melt. Top with bite size pieces of red bell pepper and avocado. Use tortilla chips to scoop up and enjoy the "nacho dip."
4. Prepare the salad.
5. Serve Skillet Nacho Dip with salad.

Prepare to Freeze Directions

Brown 1 lb. ground beef with 2 Tbsp minced onion and 1 tsp garlic powder. Drain and set aside to cool.

Open, drain and rinse 1 can of pinto beans.

Open 1 can of diced tomatoes with green chiles.

To a gallon-size plastic freezer baggie, add the following ingredients:
- Browned, cooled ground beef
- 15 oz. can pinto beans
- 10 oz. can diced tomatoes with green chiles
- 1 packet taco seasoning
- Salt and pepper

Remove as much air as possible and seal. Add label to baggie and freeze.

Freeze & Thaw Directions

Put the baggie in the freezer and freeze for up to 6 months in a fridge freezer or 12 months in a deep freezer. Thaw in the fridge overnight, or a bowl of lukewarm water for about 20 minutes, before transferring to the skillet to reheat and then top with shredded cheese and red pepper and avocado garnishes. Serve with tortilla chips.

Skillet Sloppy Joe Nachos

Yield: 4 servings
Prep Time: 10 minutes
Cook Time: 20 minutes

Ingredients

- 1 lb. ground beef
- 15 oz. can sloppy joe sauce
- 1 Tbsp ground cumin
- 1 bag tortilla chips
- 2 cups shredded Monterey Jack cheese
- Garnish: sour cream
- Side: fruit
- 1 gallon-size freezer baggie

Cooking Directions

1. Preheat the oven to 350 F.
2. Open the can of sloppy joe sauce.
3. In a large skillet, brown the ground beef. Drain and return to the skillet. Stir in the sloppy joe sauce and ground cumin. Bring to bubbling over medium low heat to allow flavors to infuse.
4. Assemble the nachos on a large, rimmed baking sheet. Add chips, then sloppy joe meat sauce, then shredded Monterey Jack cheese on top.
5. Bake in the preheated oven for 10 to 15 minutes, or until the cheese has melted. Garnish with sour cream.
6. Prepare fruit.
7. Serve Sloppy Joe Nachos with fruit.

Prepare to Freeze Directions

Brown 1 lb. ground beef. Drain and set aside to cool.

Open 1 can of sloppy joe sauce.

To a gallon-size plastic freezer baggie, add the following ingredients:
- Browned, cooled ground beef
- 15 oz. can sloppy joe sauce
- 1 Tbsp ground cumin

Remove as much air as possible and seal. Add label to baggie and freeze.

Freeze & Thaw Directions

Put the baggie in the freezer and freeze for up to 6 months in a fridge freezer or 12 months in a deep freezer. Thaw in the fridge overnight, or a bowl of lukewarm water for about 20 minutes, before transferring to the skillet to reheat. Once the meat sauce is reheated, assemble nachos and bake as directed.

Stovetop 5-Ingredient Chili

Yield:	4 servings
Prep Time:	10 minutes
Cook Time:	20 minutes

Ingredients

- 1 lb. ground beef
- 1 small white onion
- 2 - 15 oz. cans red kidney beans
- 2 - 15 oz. cans diced tomatoes & green chiles
- 2 Tbsp chili powder
- Salt and pepper
- Garnish: shredded cheese
- Side: salad
- 1 gallon-size freezer baggie

Cooking Directions

1. Chop the onion.
2. Open and drain the 2 cans of red kidney beans. Open 2 cans of diced tomatoes with green chiles.
3. In a large saucepan, brown the ground beef with salt and pepper. Drain and return to the saucepan.
4. Stir in the diced tomatoes with green chiles, drained red kidney beans, and 1 cup of hot water. Stir in the chopped onion and chili powder. Bring to bubbling and reduce heat and simmer for 10 minutes to allow flavors to mingle.
5. Prepare the salad.
6. Serve 5-Ingredient Chili with shredded cheese garnish and salad.

Prepare to Freeze Directions

Brown 1 lb. ground beef. Set aside and let cool.

Chop the white onion.

Open and drain 2 cans of red kidney beans. Open 2 cans of diced tomatoes with green chiles.

To a gallon-size plastic freezer baggie, add the following ingredients:
- Browned, cooled ground beef
- 2 - 15 oz. cans red kidney beans, drained
- 2 - 15 oz. cans diced tomatoes with green chiles
- Chopped onion
- 2 Tbsp chili powder
- Salt and pepper

Remove as much air as possible and seal. Add label to baggie and freeze.

Freeze & Thaw Directions

Put the baggie in the freezer and freeze for up to 6 months in a fridge freezer or 12 months in a deep freezer. Thaw in the fridge overnight, or a bowl of lukewarm water for about 20 minutes, before transferring to a saucepan with 1 cup of water and reheating.

Stovetop Classic Spaghetti Sauce

Yield: 4 servings
Prep Time: 10 minutes
Cook Time: 20 minutes

Ingredients

- 1 lb. ground beef
- 1 Tbsp minced onion
- 26 oz. jar spaghetti sauce
- 2 whole carrots
- 1 small zucchini
- Salt and pepper
- Side: small shell pasta
- Side: veggies
- 1 gallon-size freezer baggie

Cooking Directions

1. Cook pasta as directed.
2. Grate the zucchini. Peel and grate the carrots.
3. In a large skillet, brown the ground beef with the minced onion. Drain and return to the skillet.
4. Stir in the spaghetti sauce, grated carrots and grated zucchini and simmer for 10 to 15 minutes. Season with salt and pepper to taste.
5. Serve Classic Spaghetti Sauce with pasta and veggies.

Prepare to Freeze Directions

Brown 1 lb. ground beef with 1 Tbsp minced onion. Drain and set aside to cool.

Peel and grate 2 whole carrots. Grate 1 zucchini.

To a gallon-size plastic freezer baggie, add the following ingredients:
- Browned, cooled ground beef
- 26 oz. jar spaghetti sauce
- Peeled and grated carrots
- Grated zucchini
- Salt and pepper

Remove as much air as possible and seal. Add label to baggie and freeze.

Freeze & Thaw Directions

Put the baggie in the freezer and freeze for up to 6 months in a fridge freezer or 12 months in a deep freezer. Thaw in the fridge overnight, or a bowl of lukewarm water for about 20 minutes, before transferring to the saucepan to reheat. Serve over pasta, as directed.

Chapter 3 -
5-Ingredient Pork Recipes

Baked Apple BBQ Pork Chops

Baked Cheesy Garlic Pork Chops

Baked Chipotle Pork Chops

Baked Cranberry Mustard Pork Chops

Baked Ginger Peach Pork Chops

Baked Italian Pork Chops

Baked Peach Orange Pork Chops

Baked Penne Smoked Sausage Alfredo

Baked Salsa Pork Chops

Roasted Garlic Pork Chops

Slow Cooker Caesar Pork Chops and Potatoes

Slow Cooker Dr. Pepper Pulled Pork

Slow Cooker Italian Tortellini

Slow Cooker Raspberry Chipotle Pork with Sweet Potatoes

Slow Cooker Spicy Sausage & Peppers

Slow Cooker Sweet Chili Pork Chops

Baked Apple BBQ Pork Chops

Yield: 4 servings
Prep Time: 10 minutes
Cook Time: 35 minutes

Ingredients

- 4 boneless pork chops
- Salt and pepper
- 1/2 cup BBQ sauce
- 1/2 cup applesauce
- Side: rice
- Side: salad
- 9x13-inch disposable foil tray

Cooking Directions

1. Preheat the oven to 375 F. Lightly spray a 9x13-inch baking dish with non-stick cooking spray. Place the pork chops into the baking dish and season both sides with salt and pepper.
2. In a small mixing bowl, whisk together the applesauce and BBQ sauce. Pour over the pork chops and bake in the preheated oven for 30 to 35 minutes, or until pork chops reach 145 F. Let rest for 5 minutes before serving or slicing. Cooking time may vary depending on the thickness of the pork chops.
3. Cook the rice, as directed.
4. Prepare salad.
5. Serve Apple BBQ Pork Chops over rice with salad.

Prepare to Freeze Directions

In a small mixing bowl, whisk together 1/2 cup applesauce and 1/2 cup BBQ sauce.

To the disposable tray, add the following ingredients:
- 4 boneless pork chops
- Salt and pepper
- Prepared sauce over the pork chops

Cover with foil or lid, add label and freeze.

Freeze & Thaw Directions

Put the tray in the freezer and freeze for up to 6 months in a fridge freezer or 12 months in a deep freezer. Thaw in the fridge overnight, before transferring to the oven and baking as directed.

If baking from frozen or partially frozen, keep the dish covered tightly with foil and double the baking time. Bake until meat is cooked through.

Baked Cheesy Garlic Pork Chops

Yield:	4 servings
Prep Time:	5 minutes
Cook Time:	35 minutes

Ingredients

- 4 boneless pork chops
- Salt and pepper
- 2 Tbsp melted butter
- 2 tsp minced garlic
- 1 tsp onion powder
- 1 cup shredded cheddar cheese
- Side: dinner rolls
- Side: veggies
- 9x13-inch disposable foil tray

Cooking Directions

1. Preheat the oven to 350 F. Lightly spray a 9x13-inch baking dish with non-stick cooking spray. Place the pork chops into the baking dish and season with salt and pepper.
2. In a small bowl, stir the melted butter, minced garlic, and onion powder. Brush it onto the pork chops. Add a pinch full of shredded mild cheddar cheese onto each pork chop.
3. Bake in the preheated oven for 30 to 35 minutes, or until pork chops reach 145 F. Let rest for 5 minutes before serving or slicing. Cooking time may vary depending on the thickness of the pork chops.
4. Prepare veggies.
5. Warm the dinner rolls.
6. Serve Cheesy Garlic Pork Chops with veggies and dinner rolls.

Prepare to Freeze Directions

In a small bowl, stir 2 Tbsp melted butter, 2 tsp minced garlic, and 1 tsp onion powder.

To the disposable tray, add the following ingredients:
- 4 boneless pork chops
- Melted butter mixture, brushed onto each pork chop
- Pinch full of shredded mild cheddar, onto each pork chop

Cover with foil or lid, add label and freeze.

Freeze & Thaw Directions

Put the tray in the freezer and freeze for up to 6 months in a fridge freezer or 12 months in a deep freezer. Thaw in the fridge overnight, before transferring to the oven and baking as directed.

If baking from frozen or partially frozen, keep the dish covered tightly with foil and double the baking time. Bake until meat is cooked through.

Baked Chipotle Pork Chops

Yield: 4 servings
Prep Time: 5 minutes
Cook Time: 35 minutes

Ingredients

- 4 boneless pork chops
- Salt and pepper
- 15 oz. can diced tomatoes
- 1 tsp minced garlic
- 1 tsp ground cumin
- 1 tsp chipotle chili powder
- Side: dinner rolls
- Side: veggies
- 1 gallon-size freezer baggie

Cooking Directions

1. Preheat the oven to 350 F. Place the pork chops into a 9x13-inch baking dish and season both sides with salt and pepper.
2. In a mixing bowl, toss together the diced tomatoes with minced garlic, ground cumin and chipotle chili powder. Pour the tomatoes over the pork chops and bake in the preheated oven for 30 to 35 minutes, or until pork is cooked through. Let rest 5 minutes before serving.
3. Prepare veggies.
4. Warm the dinner rolls.
5. Serve Chipotle Pork Chops with dinner rolls and veggies.

Prepare to Freeze Directions

Open 1 can diced tomatoes.

In a mixing bowl, toss together 1 can diced tomatoes with 1 tsp minced garlic, 1 tsp ground cumin and 1 tsp chipotle chili powder.

To a gallon-size plastic freezer baggie, add the following ingredients:
- 4 boneless pork chops
- Salt and pepper
- Diced tomatoes and seasoning sauce

Remove as much air as possible and seal. Add label to baggie and freeze.

Freeze & Thaw Directions

Put the tray in the freezer and freeze for up to 6 months in a fridge freezer or 12 months in a deep freezer. Thaw in the fridge overnight, or a bowl of lukewarm water for about 20 minutes, before transferring to the baking dish and baking as directed.

If baking from frozen or partially frozen, keep the dish covered tightly with foil and double the baking time. Bake until meat is cooked through.

Baked Cranberry Mustard Pork Chops

Yield: 4 servings
Prep Time: 10 minutes
Cook Time: 35 minutes

Ingredients

- 4 boneless pork chops
- Salt and pepper
- 1/2 tsp cinnamon
- 15 oz. can whole cranberries
- 1/4 cup spicy mustard
- Side: rice
- Side: veggies
- 9x13-inch disposable foil tray

Cooking Directions

1. Preheat the oven to 375 F. Spray a 9x13-inch glass baking dish with non-stick cooking spray. and cook on low for 8 hours.
2. Place the pork chops into the baking dish and sprinkle with salt and pepper and add a dash of cinnamon on top of each chop.
3. In a small mixing bowl, combine the whole cranberries with the spicy mustard. Pour the sauce over top of the pork chops and bake in the preheated oven for 30 to 35 minutes, or until pork chops are cooked through. Cooking time may vary, depending on the thickness of the chop.
4. Serve Cranberry Mustard Pork Chops with a side of rice and veggies.

Prepare to Freeze Directions

Whisk together 15 oz. can whole cranberries sauce & 1/4 cup spicy mustard.

To the disposable tray, add the following ingredients:
- 4 boneless pork chops
- Prepared cranberry mustard sauce, directly over the pork chops

Cover each tray with foil.

Freeze & Thaw Directions

Put the tray in the freezer and freeze for up to 6 months in a fridge freezer or 12 months in a deep freezer. Thaw in the fridge overnight, before transferring to the oven and baking as directed.

If baking from frozen or partially frozen, keep the dish covered tightly with foil and double the baking time. Bake until meat is cooked through.

Baked Ginger Peach Pork Chops

Yield: 4 servings
Prep Time: 10 minutes
Cook Time: 35 minutes

Ingredients

- 4 boneless pork chops
- Salt and pepper
- 1 cup peach preserves
- 1 Tbsp sesame oil
- 1 tsp ground ginger
- Side: veggies
- Side: mashed potatoes
- 9x13-inch disposable foil tray

Cooking Directions

1. Preheat the oven to 350 F. Lightly spray a 9x13-inch baking dish with non-stick cooking spray.
2. Place the pork chops into the baking dish and season with salt and pepper.
3. In a small bowl, mix together the peach preserves, sesame oil and ground ginger. Evenly divide and coat each pork chop.
4. Bake in the preheated oven for 30 to 35 minutes, or until pork chops reach 145 F. Let rest for 5 minutes before serving or slicing. Cooking time may vary depending on the thickness of the pork chops.
5. Prepare veggies.
6. Prepare mashed potatoes.
7. Serve Ginger Peach Pork Chops with veggies and mashed potatoes.

Prepare to Freeze Directions

In a small bowl, mix together 1 cup peach preserves, 1 Tbsp sesame oil and 1 tsp ground ginger.

To the disposable tray, add the following ingredients:
- 4 boneless pork chops
- Salt and pepper
- Peach preserve mixture, directly onto each pork chops

Cover with foil or lid, add label and freeze.

Freeze & Thaw Directions

Put the tray in the freezer and freeze for up to 6 months in a fridge freezer or 12 months in a deep freezer. Thaw in the fridge overnight, before transferring to the oven and baking as directed.

If baking from frozen or partially frozen, keep the dish covered tightly with foil and double the baking time. Bake until meat is cooked through.

Baked Italian Pork Chops

Yield: 4 servings
Prep Time: 10 minutes
Cook Time: 35 minutes

Ingredients

- 4 boneless pork chops
- Salt and pepper
- 15 oz. can diced tomatoes
- 1 Tbsp Italian seasoning
- 1 tsp minced garlic
- 1 tsp minced onion
- Side: dinner rolls
- Side: salad
- 9x13-inch disposable foil tray

Cooking Directions

1. Preheat the oven to 400 F.
2. Place the pork chops into a 9x13-inch baking dish and sprinkle with salt and pepper.
3. Open and drain the diced tomatoes.
4. In a small mixing bowl, stir together the drained diced tomatoes, Italian seasoning, minced garlic and minced onion. Pour tomato-spice mixture on top of the pork chops.
5. Bake in the preheated oven for 30 to 35 minutes, or until pork chops are cooked through. Cooking time may vary depending on the thickness of the chops.
6. Prepare the salad.
7. Warm the dinner rolls.
8. Serve Baked Italian Pork Chops with salad and dinner rolls.

Prepare to Freeze Directions

Open and drain 1 can of diced tomatoes.

In a small mixing bowl, stir together the can of drained diced tomatoes, 1 Tbsp Italian seasoning, 1 tsp minced garlic, and 1 tsp minced onion.

To the disposable tray, add the following ingredients:
- 4 boneless pork chops
- Salt and pepper
- Diced tomatoes-spices mixture

Cover with foil or lid, add label and freeze.

Freeze & Thaw Directions

Put the tray in the freezer and freeze for up to 6 months in a fridge freezer or 12 months in a deep freezer. Thaw in the fridge overnight, before transferring to the oven and baking as directed.

If baking from frozen or partially frozen, keep the dish covered tightly with foil and double the baking time. Bake until meat is cooked through.

Baked Peach Orange Pork Chops

Yield: 4 servings
Prep Time: 5 minutes
Cook Time: 35 minutes

Ingredients

- 4 boneless pork chops
- Salt and pepper
- 1/4 cup peach preserves
- 1/4 cup orange marmalade
- 2 Tbsp Dijon mustard
- 1 tsp soy sauce
- Side: dinner rolls
- Side: salad
- 1 gallon-size freezer baggie

Cooking Directions

1. Preheat the oven to 350 F. Lightly grease a 9x13-inch baking dish with non-stick cooking spray.
2. Place the pork chops into the prepared baking dish. Season with salt and pepper.
3. In a small mixing bowl, combine the 1/2 cup peach preserves, 1/2 cup orange marmalade, 4 Tbsp Dijon mustard and 2 tsp soy sauce. Place directly on top of the pork chops, and bake in the preheated oven for 30 to 35 minutes, or until pork chops have cooked through. Cooking time will vary depending on the thickness of the pork chops.
4. Warm the dinner rolls.
5. Prepare the salad.
6. Serve Baked Peach Orange Pork Chops with dinner rolls and salad.

Prepare to Freeze Directions

In a small mixing bowl, combine the 1/4 cup peach preserves, 1/4 cup orange marmalade, 2 Tbsp Dijon mustard and 1 tsp soy sauce.

To a gallon-size plastic freezer baggie, add the following ingredients:
- 4 boneless pork chops
- Prepared peach-orange sauce directly onto each pork chop

Remove as much air as possible and seal. Add label to baggie and freeze.

Freeze & Thaw Directions

Put the tray in the freezer and freeze for up to 6 months in a fridge freezer or 12 months in a deep freezer. Thaw in the fridge overnight, before transferring to the baking dish and cooking as directed.

If baking from frozen or partially frozen, keep the dish covered tightly with foil and double the baking time. Bake until meat is cooked through.

Baked Penne Smoked Sausage Alfredo

Yield: 4 servings
Prep Time: 15 minutes
Cook Time: 35 minutes

Ingredients

- 16 oz. penne pasta noodles
- 16 oz. smoked pre-cooked sausage links
- 24 oz. jar alfredo sauce
- 1 cup Parmesan cheese
- Salt and pepper
- 2 cups shredded mozzarella cheese
- Side: salad
- 9x13-inch disposable foil tray

Cooking Directions

1. Preheat the oven to 400 F.
2. Cook the pasta to al dente, about 7 minutes. Drain and add to a 9x13-inch baking dish.
3. Slice the pre-cooked smoked sausage into ½-inch slices.
4. Add the sliced sausage into the baking dish with the pasta, then gently toss with the alfredo sauce and grated Parmesan cheese. Sprinkle the mozzarella cheese on top.
5. Cover and bake in the preheated oven for 15 minutes, then uncover and bake another 10 minutes.
6. Prepare the salad.
7. Serve Penne Smoked Sausage Alfredo Bake with salad.

Prepare to Freeze Directions

Slice 16 oz. pre-cooked smoked sausage into ½-inch slices.

Cook the pasta to al dente, about 7 minutes. Drain.

To the disposable tray, add the following ingredients on top of the pasta:
- Cooked pasta
- Sliced sausages
- 24 oz. jar alfredo sauce
- 1 cup grated Parmesan cheese, sprinkled on top
- Shredded mozzarella cheese, sprinkled on top

Cover with foil or lid, add label and freeze.

Freeze & Thaw Directions

Put the tray in the freezer and freeze for up to 6 months in a fridge freezer or 12 months in a deep freezer. Thaw in the fridge overnight, before transferring to the oven and baking as directed.

If baking from frozen or partially frozen, keep the dish covered tightly with foil and double the baking time. Bake until meat is cooked or warmed through.

Baked Salsa Pork Chops

Yield: 4 servings
Prep Time: 10 minutes
Cook Time: 35 minutes

Ingredients

- 4 boneless pork chops
- 1 cup red salsa
- 4 oz. can green chiles
- Salt and pepper
- Garnish: avocado slices
- Side: rice
- Side: salad
- 1 gallon-size freezer baggie

Cooking Directions

1. Preheat the oven to 350 F. Lightly grease a 9x13-inch baking dish with non-stick cooking spray.
2. Place the boneless pork chops into the prepared baking dish.
3. Pour the red salsa and green chilies around the pork chops. Season with salt and pepper.
4. Bake in the preheated oven for 30 to 35 minutes, or until pork chops have cooked through. Cooking time will vary depending on the thickness of the pork chops.
5. Cook the rice as directed.
6. Prepare salad and slice avocado garnish.
7. Serve Baked Salsa Pork Chops with avocado slices, over rice with veggies.

Prepare to Freeze Directions

To a gallon-size plastic freezer baggie, add the following ingredients:
- 4 boneless pork chops
- 1 cup red salsa
- 4 oz. can green chilies
- Salt and pepper

Remove as much air as possible and seal. Add label to baggie and freeze.

Freeze & Thaw Directions

Put the baggie in the freezer and freeze for up to 6 months in a fridge freezer or 12 months in a deep freezer. Thaw in the fridge overnight, or a bowl of lukewarm water for about 20 minutes, before transferring to the baking dish and baking as directed.

If baking from frozen or partially frozen, keep the dish covered tightly with foil and double the baking time. Bake until meat is cooked through.

Roasted Garlic Pork Chops

Yield: 4 servings
Prep Time: 5 minutes
Cook Time: 35 minutes

Ingredients

- 4 boneless pork chops
- Salt and pepper
- 2 Tbsp melted butter
- 2 Tbsp roasted garlic
- Side: dinner rolls
- Side: veggies
- 9x13-inch disposable foil tray

Cooking Directions

1. Preheat the oven to 350 F. Lightly spray a 9x13-inch baking dish with non-stick cooking spray. Place the pork chops into the baking dish and season both sides with salt and pepper.
2. In a small bowl, stir the melted butter and roasted garlic. Brush directly onto the pork chops.
3. Bake in the preheated oven for 30 to 35 minutes, or until pork chops reach 145 F. Let rest for 5 minutes before serving or slicing. Cooking time may vary depending on the thickness of the pork chops.
4. Prepare veggies.
5. Warm the dinner rolls.
6. Serve Roasted Garlic Pork Chops with veggies and dinner rolls.

Prepare to Freeze Directions

In a small bowl, stir 2 Tbsp melted butter and 2 Tbsp roasted garlic.

To the disposable tray, add the following ingredients:

- 4 boneless pork chops
- Melted butter mixture, brushed onto each pork chop

Cover with foil or lid, add label and freeze.

Freeze & Thaw Directions

Put the baggie in the freezer and freeze for up to 6 months in a fridge freezer or 12 months in a deep freezer. Thaw in the fridge overnight, before transferring to the oven and baking as directed.

If baking from frozen or partially frozen, keep the dish covered tightly with foil and double the baking time. Bake until meat is cooked through.

Slow Cooker Caesar Pork Chops and Potatoes

Yield: 4 servings
Prep Time: 5 minutes
Cook Time: 4 hours in slow cooker

Ingredients

- 4 boneless pork chops
- Salt and pepper
- 1 packet Italian seasoning
- 2 lb. bag fingerling potatoes
- 1 cup Caesar salad dressing
- Garnish: shredded Parmesan cheese
- Side: salad
- 1 gallon-size freezer baggie

Cooking Directions

1. Open the Italian seasoning packet and sprinkle it into a shallow dish or plate. Press both sides of the pork chops into the seasoning and then place into the base of the slow cooker. Season with a little salt and pepper and then add the fingerling potatoes around the pork chops. Drizzle the Caesar dressing over the pork chops and potatoes.
2. Set the slow cooker on low and cook for 4 hours.
3. Prepare the salad.
4. Serve Slow Cooker Caesar Pork Chops and Potatoes with shredded Parmesan garnish and salad.

Prepare to Freeze Directions

Open 1 Italian seasoning packet and sprinkle into a shallow dish or plate. Press both sides of the pork chops into the seasoning.

To a gallon-size plastic freezer baggie, add the following ingredients:
- 4 seasoned boneless pork chops
- Salt and pepper
- 2 lb. bag fingerling potatoes
- 1 cup Caesar salad dressing

Remove as much air as possible and seal. Add label to baggie and freeze.

Freeze & Thaw Directions

Put the baggie in the freezer and freeze for up to 6 months in a fridge freezer or 12 months in a deep freezer. Thaw completely in the fridge overnight, and then transfer to the slow cooker and cook on low for 4 hours.

If slow cooking from frozen or partially frozen, add ½ cup of water or chicken stock to the slow cooker insert and change the slow cook time to low for 8 hours.

Slow Cooker Dr. Pepper Pulled Pork

Yield: 4 servings
Prep Time: 10 minutes
Cook Time: 8 hours in slow cooker

Ingredients

- 2 lb. pork shoulder roast
- 1/2 small red onion
- Salt and pepper
- 12 oz. can Dr. Pepper
- 2 cups BBQ sauce
- 4 hamburger buns
- Side: Coleslaw salad kit
- Side: chips
- 1 gallon-size freezer baggie

Cooking Directions

1. Thinly slice the red onion.
2. Place the pork roast and red onion slices in the base of the slow cooker and sprinkle with salt and pepper. Pour the Dr. Pepper and BBQ sauce over the pork roast. Set the slow cooker on low and cook for 8 hours.
3. Prepare the coleslaw salad just before serving.
4. Once the pork roast is cooked, shred the meat with 2 forks and toss with the sauce. Spoon shredded pork onto hamburger buns and top with Coleslaw.
5. Serve Slow Cooker Dr. Pepper Pulled Pork with chips.

Prepare to Freeze Directions

Thinly slice 1/2 small red onion.

To a gallon-size plastic freezer baggie, add the following ingredients:
- 2 lb. pork shoulder roast
- Red onion slices
- Salt and pepper
- 12 oz. can Dr. Pepper
- 2 cups BBQ sauce

Remove as much air as possible and seal. Add label to baggie and freeze.

Freeze & Thaw Directions

Put the baggie in the freezer and freeze for up to 6 months in a fridge freezer or 12 months in a deep freezer. Thaw in the fridge overnight, or a bowl of lukewarm water for about 20 minutes, before transferring to the slow cooker and cooking on low for 8 hours. Shred the pork and assemble sandwiches as directed.

Slow Cooker Italian Tortellini

Yield: 4 servings
Prep Time: 10 minutes
Cook Time: 1 hour in slow cooker

Ingredients

- 1 lb. ground Italian sausage
- Salt and pepper
- 20 oz. fresh or frozen tortellini
- 26 oz. jar marinara sauce
- 1 cup beef stock
- 1 Tbsp Italian seasoning
- 1 cup grated Parmesan cheese
- 1 cup shredded mozzarella cheese
- Side: salad
- 1 gallon-size freezer baggie

Cooking Directions

1. In a skillet, brown the ground Italian sausage, then drain.
2. Place the browned Italian sausage into the base of the slow cooker and add the tortellini (fresh or frozen), marinara, beef stock, salt, pepper, and Italian seasoning. Gently stir through.
3. Set the slow cooker on low and cook for 1 hour. At the end of the cooking cycle, stir the grated Parmesan cheese into the sauce, and then top with shredded mozzarella cheese.
4. Prepare salad.
5. Serve Slow Cooker Italian Tortellini with side salad.

Prepare to Freeze Directions

In a large skillet, brown 1 lb. ground Italian sausage, then drain.

To a gallon-size plastic freezer baggie, add the following ingredients:
- Browned sausage
- 20 oz. box fresh or frozen tortellini
- 26 oz. jar marinara sauce
- 1 cup beef stock
- 1 Tbsp Italian seasoning
- Salt and pepper
- Do NOT add the 2 cheeses to the freezer baggie.

Remove as much air as possible and seal. Add label to baggie and freeze.

Freeze & Thaw Directions

Put the baggie in the freezer and freeze for up to 6 months in a fridge freezer or 12 months in a deep freezer. Thaw in the fridge overnight, or a bowl of lukewarm water for about 20 minutes, before transferring to the slow cooker and cooking on low for 1 hour. Add cheese, as directed, before serving.

Slow Cooker Raspberry Chipotle Pork with Sweet Potatoes

Yield: 4 servings
Prep Time: 10 minutes
Cook Time: 8 hours in slow cooker

Ingredients

- 2 lb. pork shoulder roast
- Salt and pepper
- 4 medium sweet potatoes
- 1 lb. bag baby carrots
- 1 cup raspberry chipotle sauce
- Side: salad
- 1 gallon-size freezer baggie

Cooking Directions

1. Peel and dice the sweet potatoes.
2. Add the pork roast to the base of the slow cooker and sprinkle with salt and pepper. Spread the diced sweet potatoes and baby carrots around and on top of the pork roast. Pour the Raspberry Chipotle sauce over the top of the meat and veggies.
3. Set the slow cooker on low and cook for 8 hours.
4. Serve Slow Cooker Raspberry Chipotle Pork Roast with Sweet Potatoes and Carrots and side salad.

Prepare to Freeze Directions

Peel and dice 4 medium sweet potatoes.

To a gallon-size plastic freezer baggie, add the following ingredients:

- 2 lb. pork shoulder roast
- Salt and pepper
- Diced sweet potatoes
- 1 lb. bag baby carrots
- 1 cup raspberry chipotle sauce

Remove as much air as possible and seal. Add label to baggie and freeze.

Freeze & Thaw Directions

Put the baggie in the freezer and freeze for up to 6 months in a fridge freezer or 12 months in a deep freezer. Thaw in the fridge overnight, or a bowl of lukewarm water for about 20 minutes, before transferring to the slow cooker and cooking on low for 8 hours.

Slow Cooker Spicy Sausage & Peppers

Yield:	4 servings
Prep Time:	5 minutes
Cook Time:	8 hours in slow cooker

Ingredients

- 1 lb. pork sausage links
- 15 oz. can diced tomatoes
- 4 oz. can green chiles
- 10 oz. bag frozen peppers and onions
- Salt and pepper
- Side: rice
- 1 gallon-size freezer baggie

Cooking Directions

1. Slice or cut the sausage links into ½-inch slices. Place the slices into the base of the slow cooker insert.
2. Pour the diced tomatoes, diced green chilies, and bag of frozen peppers and onions blend over the top. Mix well. Set the slow cooker on low and cook for 8 hours. Season with salt and pepper to taste.
3. Cook rice, as directed.
4. Serve Slow Cooker Spicy Sausage and Peppers over rice.

Prepare to Freeze Directions

Slice or cut 1 lb. sausage links into ½-inch slices.

Open 1 can of diced tomatoes. Open 1 can of diced green chilies.

To a gallon-size plastic freezer baggie, add the following ingredients:
- Sliced sausage
- 15 oz. can diced tomatoes with juices
- 4 oz. can diced green chilies
- 10 oz. bag frozen pepper and onion blend
- Salt and pepper

Remove as much air as possible and seal. Add label to baggie and freeze.

Freeze & Thaw Directions

Put the baggie in the freezer and freeze for up to 6 months in a fridge freezer or 12 months in a deep freezer. Thaw in the fridge overnight, or a bowl of lukewarm water for about 20 minutes, before transferring to the slow cooker and cooking on low for 8 hours.

Slow Cooker Sweet Chili Pork Chops

Yield: 4 servings
Prep Time: 5 minutes
Cook Time: 8 hours in slow cooker

Ingredients

- 4 boneless pork chops
- Salt and pepper
- 1/4 cup sweet Thai chili sauce
- Side: rice
- Side: veggies
- 1 gallon-size freezer baggie

Cooking Directions

1. Add the pork chops to the base of the slow cooker and season with salt and pepper. Brush the sweet Thai chili sauce onto each pork chop.
2. Note: if your slow cooker "runs hot" or tends to dry out meats, add ½ cup of water into the base with the pork chops.
3. Set the slow cooker on low and cook for 8 hours.
4. Cook the rice, as directed.
5. Prepare veggies.
6. Serve Slow Cooker Sweet Chili Pork Chops with veggies and rice.

Prepare to Freeze Directions

To a gallon size freezer baggie, add the following ingredients:

- 4 boneless pork chops
- Salt and pepper
- 1/4 cup Sweet Thai chili sauce, brushed onto the pork chops

Remove as much air as possible, add label and freeze.

Freeze & Thaw Directions

Put the baggie in the freezer and freeze for up to 6 months in a fridge freezer or 12 months in a deep freezer. Thaw in the fridge overnight, before transferring to the slow cooker and cooking as directed.

Chapter 4 –
5-Ingredient Seafood Recipes

Baked Buttery Salmon

Yield: 4 servings
Prep Time: 5 minutes*
Cook Time: 20 minutes

Ingredients

- 1 lb. salmon fillet
- 4 Tbsp butter
- 2 tsp herb seasoning blend
- Side: rice
- Side: veggies
- 1 gallon-size freezer baggie

Cooking Directions

1. Set the butter on the counter to soften.*
2. Cook rice, as directed.
3. Combine the softened butter with the seasoning blend to make a compound.
4. Preheat the oven to 400 F.
5. Cut salmon fillet into 4 portions. Place the fillets in a small baking dish and season with salt and pepper. Add a dollop of the butter compound onto each piece of salmon fillet.
6. Bake in the preheated oven for 15 to 20 minutes, or until salmon is no longer pink in the middle. Cooking time may vary depending on the thickness of salmon. Remove skin from cooked salmon.
7. Prepare veggies.
8. Serve Buttery Salmon with rice and veggies.

Prepare to Freeze Directions

Cut 1 lb. of salmon fillet into 4 portions.

Let the 4 Tbsp butter soften and then combine it with 2 tsp seasoning blend to make a compound.

To a gallon-size plastic freezer baggie, add the following ingredients:
- 4 salmon fillets
- Salt and pepper
- Dollop of butter compound on each salmon

Remove as much air as possible and seal. Add label to baggie and freeze.

Freeze & Thaw Directions

Put the baggie in the freezer and freeze for up to 6 months in a fridge freezer or 12 months in a deep freezer. Thaw the salmon completely, before transferring the salmon and butter compound to the baking dish. Bake as directed.

Baked Chili Lime Salmon

Yield: 4 servings
Prep Time: 15 minutes
Cook Time: 20 minutes

Ingredients

- 1 lb. salmon fillet
- Salt and pepper
- 3 Tbsp sweet Thai chili sauce
- 2 Tbsp lime juice
- 1 tsp minced garlic
- Side: rice
- Garnish: lime wedges
- Side: salad or veggies
- 1 gallon-size freezer baggie

Cooking Directions

1. Preheat the oven to 400 F. Lightly grease an 8x8-inch baking dish with non-stick cooking spray.
2. Cut the salmon into 4 portions and place in the prepared dish.
3. In a small mixing bowl, whisk together the sweet chili sauce, lime juice, and garlic. Pour over the salmon.
4. Bake in the preheated oven for 15 to 20 minutes, or until cooked through. Cooking time will depend on the thickness of the salmon. Remove skin from cooked salmon.
5. Cook the rice as directed on the package.
6. Prepare salad or veggies.
7. Serve Baked Chili Lime Salmon with a side of dinner rolls and salad or veggies.

Prepare to Freeze Directions

Cut the salmon fillet into 4 portions.

In a small bowl, whisk together 3 Tbsp sweet chili sauce, 2 Tbsp lime juice, and 1 tsp minced garlic.

To a gallon-size plastic freezer baggie, add the following ingredients:
- 4 salmon fillets
- Salt and pepper
- Sweet chili lime sauce, brushed directly onto the salmon

Remove as much air as possible and seal. Add label to baggie and freeze.

Freeze & Thaw Directions

Put the baggie in the freezer and freeze for up to 6 months in a fridge freezer or 12 months in a deep freezer. Thaw the salmon completely, before transferring the salmon to the baking dish, and baking as directed.

Baked Ginger Peach Salmon

Yield: 4 servings
Prep Time: 5 minutes
Cook Time: 20 minutes

Ingredients

- 1 lb. salmon fillet
- 1 Tbsp sesame oil
- 1 tsp ground ginger
- Salt and pepper
- 6 oz. jar peach preserves
- Side: veggies
- Side: rice
- 1 gallon-size freezer baggie

Cooking Directions

1. Cook rice, as directed.
2. Preheat the oven to 400 F.
3. Cut salmon fillet into 4 portions. Place in a small baking dish. Drizzle the sesame oil over the salmon. Sprinkle ground ginger, salt and pepper onto each piece of salmon. Add a large spoonful of peach preserves onto each piece of salmon and carefully spread it over the salmon.
4. Bake in the preheated oven for 15 to 20 minutes, or until salmon is no longer pink in the middle. Cooking time will depend on the thickness of the salmon. Remove skin from cooked salmon.
5. Prepare veggies.
6. Serve Ginger Peach Salmon with a side of rice and veggies.

Prepare to Freeze Directions

Cut the salmon fillet into 4 portions.

To a gallon-size plastic freezer baggie, add the following ingredients:
- 4 salmon fillets
- 1 Tbsp sesame oil
- 1 tsp ground ginger
- Salt and pepper
- Spoonful of peach preserves, spread onto each piece of salmon

Remove as much air as possible and seal. Add label to baggie and freeze.

Freeze & Thaw Directions

Put the baggie in the freezer and freeze for up to 6 months in a fridge freezer or 12 months in a deep freezer. Thaw the salmon completely, before transferring the salmon to the baking dish, and baking as directed.

Baked Honey Mustard Salmon

Yield: 4 servings
Prep Time: 10 minutes*
Cook Time: 20 minutes

Ingredients

- 1 lb. salmon fillet
- Salt and pepper
- 3 Tbsp honey
- 3 Tbsp Dijon mustard
- 1 Tbsp apple cider vinegar
- Side: salad
- Side: dinner rolls
- 1 gallon-size freezer baggie

Cooking Directions

1. In a small mixing bowl, whisk together the honey, Dijon mustard and apple cider vinegar.
2. Cut salmon fillet into 4 portions. Place salmon fillets into a baking dish and season with salt and pepper. Pour the honey mustard marinade over the salmon. Let marinate for at least 30 minutes in the fridge.*
3. Preheat the oven to 400 F.
4. Bake in the preheated for 15 to 20 minutes, or until salmon is cooked through. Cooking time may vary depending on thickness of the fillets. Remove skin from cooked salmon.
5. Prepare salad.
6. Warm the dinner rolls.
7. Serve Baked Honey Mustard Salmon with salad and dinner rolls.

Prepare to Freeze Directions

In a small mixing bowl, whisk together 3 Tbsp honey, 3 Tbsp Dijon mustard, and 1 Tbsp apple cider vinegar.

Cut the salmon fillet into 4 portions.

To a gallon-size plastic freezer baggie, add the following ingredients:
- 4 salmon fillets
- Salt and pepper
- Prepared honey mustard sauce, directly onto each salmon fillet

Remove as much as air as possible and seal.

Freeze & Thaw Directions

Put the baggie in the freezer and freeze for up to 6 months in a fridge freezer or 12 months in a deep freezer. Thaw the salmon completely, before transferring the salmon to the baking dish, and baking as directed.

Baked Jamaican Jerk Salmon Foil Packs

Yield: 4 servings
Prep Time: 5 minutes
Cook Time: 20 minutes

Ingredients

- 1 lb. salmon fillet
- Salt and pepper
- 1 Tbsp Jerk or Caribbean spice
- Garnish: pico de gallo
- Side: salad
- 1 gallon-size freezer baggie

Cooking Directions

1. Cook rice, as directed.
2. Preheat the oven to 400 F.
3. Cut salmon fillet into 4 portions.
4. Place each salmon filet on a piece of foil that is large enough to wrap around the salmon.
5. Season each salmon filet with salt and pepper. Generously sprinkle the Jerk seasoning onto each salmon fillet, coating it well.
6. Bake in the preheated oven for 15 to 20 minutes, or until salmon is no longer pink in the middle. Cooking time may vary depending on thickness of the fillets. Remove skin from cooked salmon.
7. Prepare the salad.
8. Serve Jamaican Jerk Salmon with side salad and a pico de gallo garnish on each fillet.

Prepare to Freeze Directions

Cut the salmon fillet into 4 portions.

Set up 4 large pieces of foil.

To each piece of foil, add the following ingredients:
- 1 salmon fillet
- Pinch of salt and pepper onto each salmon piece
- 2 Tbsp Jerk seasoning, evenly divided and coating each salmon fillet well

Wrap foil tightly around the salmon. Add the foil packs into a gallon-size plastic freezer baggie. Add label to baggie and freeze.

Freeze & Thaw Directions

Put the baggie in the freezer and freeze for up to 6 months in a fridge freezer or 12 months in a deep freezer. Thaw the salmon completely, before transferring the salmon packets to the oven, and baking as directed.

Baked Lemon Dill Salmon

Yield: 4 servings
Prep Time: 10 minutes
Cook Time: 20 minutes

Ingredients

- 1 lb. salmon fillet
- Salt and pepper
- 2 small lemons
- 2 tsp fresh dill
- Side: veggies
- Side: rice
- 1 gallon-size freezer baggie

Cooking Directions

1. Preheat the oven to 400 F. Lightly grease a 9x13-inch baking dish with non-stick cooking spray.
2. Slice lemons in half. Finely chop the fresh dill.
3. Cut salmon fillet into 4 portions.
4. Place the 4 salmon fillets into the baking dish, skin side down. Sprinkle each with little salt and pepper over the top. Drizzle juice from the lemon halves over the salmon pieces. Then, slice the squeezed lemon halves and place on top of the salmon. Place fresh chopped dill sprigs on salmon.
5. Bake in the preheated oven for 15 to 20 minutes, or until salmon is cooked through. Cooking time will vary depending on the thickness of the salmon fillets. Remove skin from cooked salmon.
6. Cook rice as directed on the package.
7. Prepare veggies.
8. Serve Baked Lemon Dill Salmon with rice and veggies.

Prepare to Freeze Directions

Cut the salmon fillet into 4 portions.

Slice 2 lemons.

Finely chop 2 tsp fresh dill.

To a gallon-size plastic freezer baggie, add the following ingredients:
- 4 salmon fillets
- Salt and pepper
- Lemon slices
- Chopped dill

Remove as much air as possible and seal. Add label to baggie and freeze.

Freeze & Thaw Directions

Put the baggie in the freezer and freeze for up to 6 months in a fridge freezer or 12 months in a deep freezer. Thaw the salmon completely, before transferring the salmon to the baking dish, and baking as directed.

Baked Lemon Pepper Salmon

Yield: 4 servings
Prep Time: 5 minutes
Cook Time: 20 minutes

Ingredients

- 1 lb salmon fillet
- 1 Tbsp lemon pepper seasoning
- 1 lemon
- Side: veggies
- Side: rice
- 1 gallon-size freezer baggie

Cooking Directions

1. Cook rice, as directed.
2. Preheat the oven to 400 F. Spray a 9x13-inch baking dish with non-stick cooking spray.
3. Cut salmon fillet into 4 portions. Place the salmon fillets into the prepared baking dish. Cut the lemon in half and squeeze the juice into the salmon fillets. Then sprinkle with lemon pepper seasoning on top.
4. Bake in the preheated oven for 15 to 20 minutes, or until salmon is no longer pink in the middle. Cooking time will vary depending on the thickness of the salmon fillets. Remove skin from cooked salmon.
5. Prepare veggies.
6. Serve Baked Lemon Pepper Salmon with a side of rice and veggies.

Prepare to Freeze Directions

Cut 1 lbs. of salmon fillet into 4 portions.

Halve 1 lemon.

To a gallon-size plastic freezer baggie, add the following ingredients:
- 4 salmon fillets
- Juice from the lemons
- 1 Tbsp lemon pepper seasoning, evenly divided and directly on top of salmon fillets in baggie

Remove as much air as possible and seal. Add label to baggie and freeze.

Freeze & Thaw Directions

Put the baggie in the freezer and freeze for up to 6 months in a fridge freezer or 12 months in a deep freezer. Thaw the salmon completely, before transferring the salmon to the baking dish, and baking as directed.

Baked Maple Dijon Salmon

Yield: 4 servings
Prep Time: 15 minutes
Cook Time: 20 minutes

Ingredients

- 1 lb. salmon fillet
- Salt and pepper
- 4 Tbsp maple syrup
- 4 Tbsp Dijon mustard
- Side: dinner rolls
- Side: salad or veggies
- 1 gallon-size freezer baggie

Cooking Directions

1. Preheat the oven to 400 F. Lightly grease 9x13-inch baking dish with non-stick cooking spray.
2. Cut salmon fillet into 4 portions, and place in the prepared baking dish.
3. In a small mixing bowl, whisk together the maple syrup and the Dijon mustard. Pour over the salmon fillets.
4. Bake in the preheated oven for 15 to 20 minutes, or until cooked through. Cooking time will depend on the thickness of the salmon. Remove skin from cooked salmon.
5. Warm the dinner rolls.
6. Prepare salad or veggies.
7. Serve Maple Dijon Salmon with a side of dinner rolls and salad or veggies.

Prepare to Freeze Directions

Cut the salmon fillet into 4 portions.

Whisk together 4 Tbsp maple syrup and 4 Tbsp Dijon mustard in a small bowl.

To a gallon-size plastic freezer baggie, add the following ingredients:
- 4 salmon fillets
- Salt and pepper
- Prepared Maple-Dijon sauce, directly onto the salmon fillets
- Remove as much air as possible and seal. Add label to baggie and freeze.

Freeze & Thaw Directions

Put the baggie in the freezer and freeze for up to 6 months in a fridge freezer or 12 months in a deep freezer. Thaw the salmon completely, before transferring the salmon to the baking dish, and baking as directed.

Grilled Cajun Salmon

Yield: 4 servings
Prep Time: 5 minutes*
Cook Time: 15 minutes

Ingredients

- 1 lb. salmon fillet
- Salt and pepper
- 2 Tbsp butter
- 1 Tbsp paprika
- 1 tsp garlic powder
- 1 tsp onion powder
- 1/2 tsp cayenne pepper
- Side: salad
- Side: fruit
- 1 gallon-size freezer baggie

Cooking Directions

1. Melt the butter.
2. In a small mixing bowl, combine the melted butter with the paprika, garlic powder, onion powder and cayenne pepper.
3. Cut salmon fillet into 4 portions. Place in a small baking dish and season with salt and pepper. Pour the melted butter-spice mixture directly onto the salmon. *Let sit for at least 30 minutes in the fridge.
4. Preheat the grill. Grill salmon, skin side down over direct heat for 10 to 15 minutes, or until cooked through. Grilling time will vary depending on the thickness of the salmon fillet and heat on the grill. Discard excess marinade.
5. Prepare the salad and fruit.
6. Serve Grilled Cajun Salmon over salad with a side of fruit.

Prepare to Freeze Directions

Cut the salmon fillet into 4 portions.

Melt 2 Tbsp butter.

In a small mixing bowl, combine the melted butter with 1 Tbsp paprika, 1 tsp garlic powder, 1 tsp onion powder and 1/2 tsp cayenne pepper.

To a gallon-size plastic freezer baggie, add the following ingredients:
- 4 salmon fillets
- Salt and pepper
- Butter-spice mixture

Remove as much air as possible and seal. Add label to baggie and freeze.

Freeze & Thaw Directions

Put the baggie in the freezer and freeze for up to 6 months in a fridge freezer or 12 months in a deep freezer. Thaw completely in the fridge overnight, before transferring the salmon and marinade to the grill. Grill over direct heat as directed. Discard excess marinade.

Grilled Peach BBQ Salmon

Yield:	4 servings
Prep Time:	5 minutes*
Cook Time:	15 minutes

Ingredients

- 1 lb. salmon fillet
- Salt and pepper
- 1 cup BBQ sauce
- 15 oz. can sliced peaches
- 1 tsp minced garlic
- Side: salad
- Side: fruit
- 1 gallon-size freezer baggie

Cooking Directions

1. Open and drain the juices from the peaches. Cut 4 slices into bite-size pieces. (Set aside the remaining peach slices, to serve as a side dish.)
2. In a small mixing bowl, combine the BBQ sauce, diced peaches, and minced garlic.
3. Cut salmon fillet into 4 portions. Place in a small baking dish and season with salt and pepper. Pour the BBQ-peach sauce over the salmon. Let marinate for at least 30 minutes.*
4. Preheat the grill. Place the salmon and sauce onto the grill and brush additional sauce over the top. Discard excess marinade/sauce.
5. Grill salmon, skin side down over direct heat for 12 to 15 minutes, or until cooked through. Grilling time will vary depending on the thickness of the salmon fillet and heat level of the grill. Remove skin from cooked salmon.
6. Prepare the salad and fruit.
7. Serve Grilled Peach BBQ Salmon with side salad and fruit.

Prepare to Freeze Directions

Cut 1 lb. of salmon fillet into 4 portions.

Open and drain 1 can of sliced peaches. Drain well and cut 4 peach slices into bite-size pieces. In a small mixing bowl, combine 1 cup BBQ sauce, the diced peaches, and 1 tsp minced garlic.

To a gallon-size plastic freezer baggie, add the following ingredients:
- 4 salmon fillets
- Salt and pepper
- Prepared BBQ-peach sauce, directly onto the salmon

Remove as much air as possible and seal. Add label to baggie and freeze.

Freeze & Thaw Directions

Put the baggie in the freezer and freeze for up to 6 months in a fridge freezer or 12 months in a deep freezer. Thaw completely in the fridge overnight, before transferring the salmon and marinade to the grill. Grill over direct heat as directed. Discard excess marinade.

Grilled Pesto Salmon Foil Packs

Yield: 4 servings
Prep Time: 5 minutes
Cook Time: 20 minutes

Ingredients

- 1 lb. salmon fillet
- Salt and pepper
- 8 oz. jar pesto
- 1 cup shredded mozzarella cheese
- Side: salad
- Side: rice
- 1 gallon-size freezer baggie

Cooking Directions

1. Cook rice, as directed.
2. Preheat the grill.
3. Cut salmon fillet into 4 portions.
4. Place each salmon filet on a piece of foil that's large enough to wrap around the salmon.
5. Season each salmon filet with salt and pepper. Spread the pesto directly onto the salmon, and then sprinkle the shredded mozzarella cheese on top.
6. Grill around 400 F for 15 to 20 minutes, or until salmon is no longer pink in the middle. Grilling time will vary depending on the thickness of the salmon fillet and heat level of the grill. Remove skin from cooked salmon.
7. Prepare the salad.
8. Serve Pesto Salmon with side salad and rice.

Prepare to Freeze Directions

Cut 1 lb. of salmon fillet into 4 portions.

Set up 4 large pieces of foil.

To each piece of foil, add the following ingredients:
- 1 individual portion of salmon filet
- Salt and pepper
- Dollop of pesto, spread directly onto each salmon portion
- Pinchful of shredded mozzarella cheese onto each piece of salmon

Wrap foil tightly around the chicken and veggies. Add foil packs into a gallon-size plastic freezer baggie. Add label to baggie and freeze.

Freeze & Thaw Directions

Put the baggie in the freezer and freeze for up to 6 months in a fridge freezer or 12 months in a deep freezer. Thaw completely in the fridge, before grilling as directed.

Skillet Garlic Butter Shrimp

Yield: 4 servings
Prep Time: 10 minutes
Cook Time: 15 minutes

Ingredients

- 2 lbs. peeled, deveined shrimp
- 1/4 cup chicken stock
- 2 Tbsp lemon juice
- 6 Tbsp butter
- 2 Tbsp minced garlic
- Salt and pepper
- Garnish: chopped parsley
- Side: pasta
- Side: salad
- 1 gallon-size freezer baggie

Cooking Directions

1. Heat a large skillet over medium high heat and melt half of the butter. Then whisk in the chicken stock, lemon juice, and shrimp. Bring to bubbling, and stir often. After the shrimp begins to turn pink, add in the remaining butter and minced garlic, and then cook for 5 to 7 minutes, until the sauce is smooth. Stir often. Remove from heat immediately to prevent over-cooking the sauce.
2. Cook the pasta.
3. Prepare the salad.
4. Serve Garlic Butter Shrimp over pasta with side salad.

Prepare to Freeze Directions

To a gallon-size plastic freezer baggie, add the following ingredients:
- 2 lbs. peeled deveined shrimp
- 1/4 cup chicken stock
- 2 Tbsp lemon juice
- 6 Tbsp butter (does not need to be melted)
- 2 Tbsp minced garlic

Remove as much air as possible and seal. Add label to baggie and freeze.

Freeze & Thaw Directions

Put the baggie in the freezer and freeze for up to 6 months in a fridge freezer or 12 months in a deep freezer. Thaw completely in the fridge overnight, before transferring to the skillet and sauteing all ingredients together, until sauce is smooth and shrimp is pink and cooked through.

Chapter 5 - Freezer Meal Plan #1

Slow Cooker Ranch Chicken Tacos
Slow Cooker Garlic Parmesan Chicken
Baked Sweet Chili Chicken
Buffalo Chicken Nachos
Slow Cooker BBQ Chicken Street Tacos

1. Slow Cooker Ranch Chicken Tacos

Yield: 4 servings
Active Time: 10 minutes . Cook Time: 8 hours in slow cooker

Recipe is written to make a single meal. Assembly Prep Directions & Shopping Lists will both contain directions and ingredients to make 2 meals, based on the number of servings you selected.

** This ingredient is used on the day you cook this meal. It is not added at the time you assemble and prepare your meals for the freezer.

Ingredients for Single Meal

- 4 - small boneless chicken breasts
- 1/2 - cup(s) chicken stock
- 1 - packet(s) ranch dressing mix
- 1 - packet(s) taco seasoning
- - Salt and pepper
- 8 - flour tortillas**
- Garnish: - coleslaw**
- Garnish: - Ranch salad dressing**
- Side: - salad**
- 1 - gallon-size freezer baggie(s)

Cooking Directions for Single Meal

5. Place the chicken breasts in the base of the slow cooker. Season with salt and pepper.
6. In a small mixing bowl, whisk the chicken stock and Ranch dressing mix together and pour over the chicken. Sprinkle the taco seasoning on top.
7. Set on low and cook for 8 hours. Once cooked, strain off excess liquid and shred the chicken into the sauce. Season with salt and pepper as needed. Assemble tacos with shredded chicken, coleslaw and Ranch dressing into tortillas.
8. Prepare the salad.
9. Serve Slow Cooker Ranch Chicken Tacos with coleslaw garnish and side salad.

Assembly Prep Directions for 2 Meals

To each gallon-size plastic freezer baggie, add the following ingredients:

- 4 boneless chicken breasts
- 1/2 cup chicken stock
- 1 packet Ranch dressing mix
- 1 packet taco seasoning
- Salt and pepper

Remove as much air as possible and seal. Add label to baggie and freeze.

Freeze & Thaw Instructions: *Put baggie in the freezer and freeze up to 6 months in fridge freezer or 12 months in a deep freezer. Thaw in the fridge overnight, or a warm bowl of water for about 20 minutes, before transferring to the slow cooker and cooking on low for 8 hours.*

Dairy-Free Modifications: *Recipe is dairy-free when made with dairy-free Ranch dressing and mix.*

Gluten-Free Modifications: *Recipe is gluten-free if made with gluten-free Ranch and taco seasonings.*

2. Slow Cooker Garlic Parmesan Chicken

Yield: 4 servings
Active Time: 10 minutes . Cook Time: 8 hours in slow cooker

Recipe is written to make a single meal. Assembly Prep Directions & Shopping Lists will both contain directions and ingredients to make 2 meals, based on the number of servings you selected.

** This ingredient is used on the day you cook this meal. It is not added at the time you assemble and prepare your meals for the freezer.

Ingredients for Single Meal

- 4 - small boneless chicken breasts
- 2 - lb(s) baby potatoes
- 3 - Tbsp melted butter
- 4 - tsp minced garlic
- 1 - tsp dried thyme
- - Salt and pepper
- Garnish: - shredded Parmesan cheese**
- Side: - veggies**
- 1 - gallon-size freezer baggie(s)

Cooking Directions for Single Meal

1. Melt the butter and stir in the minced garlic and thyme.
2. Place the chicken breasts and baby potatoes (do not cut) in the base of the slow cooker and pour the melted butter sauce over the top. Season with salt and pepper.
3. Set on low and cook for 8 hours.
4. Prepare veggies.
5. Serve Slow Cooker Garlic Parmesan Chicken with shredded Parmesan cheese garnish and side of veggies.

Assembly Prep Directions for 2 Meals

Melt 6 Tbsp butter and then stir in 8 tsp minced garlic and 2 tsp dried thyme.

To each gallon-size plastic freezer baggie, add the following ingredients:
- 4 boneless chicken breasts
- 1 - 2 lb. bag baby potatoes
- Half of the melted butter sauce

Remove as much air as possible and seal. Add label to baggie and freeze.

Freeze & Thaw Instructions: *Put baggie in the freezer and freeze up to 6 months in fridge freezer or 12 months in a deep freezer. Thaw in the fridge overnight, or a warm bowl of water for about 20 minutes, before transferring to the slow cooker and cooking on low for 8 hours.*

Dairy-Free Modifications: *Recipe is dairy-free when made with dairy-free margarine and you skip the Parmesan garnish.*

Gluten-Free Modifications: *Recipe is gluten-free when served with gluten-free sides.*

3. Baked Sweet Chili Chicken

Yield: 4 servings
Active Time: 10 minutes . Cook Time: 55 minutes

Recipe is written to make a single meal. Assembly Prep Directions & Shopping Lists will both contain directions and ingredients to make 2 meals, based on the number of servings you selected.

** This ingredient is used on the day you cook this meal. It is not added at the time you assemble and prepare your meals for the freezer.

Ingredients for Single Meal

- 4 - small boneless chicken breasts
- - Salt and pepper
- 1 - cup(s) sweet Thai chili sauce
- 3 - Tbsp soy sauce
- Side: - rice**
- Side: - veggies**
- 1 - 9x13 disposable foil tray(s)

Cooking Directions for Single Meal

1. Preheat the oven to 400 F. Place the chicken breasts into baking dish and season with salt and pepper.
2. In a small mixing bowl, whisk together the sweet Thai chili sauce and soy sauce. Pour over the top of the chicken, and spoon any that falls off the chicken, back on top. The sauce will glaze onto the chicken as it bakes, so you want the chicken covered on top by the sauce.
3. Bake in the preheated oven for 50 to 55 minutes, or until chicken is cooked through.
4. Cook the rice, as directed. Prepare the veggies.
5. Serve Baked Sweet Chili Chicken with rice and veggies.

Assembly Prep Directions for 2 Meals

In a small mixing bowl, whisk together 2 cups sweet Thai chili sauce and 6 Tbsp soy sauce.

To each disposable tray, add the following ingredients:
- 4 small boneless chicken breasts
- Salt and pepper onto the chicken
- Half of the prepared sauce, directly on the chicken

Cover with foil or lid, add label and freeze.

Freeze & Thaw Instructions: *Put tray in the freezer and freeze up to 6 months in fridge freezer or 12 months in a deep freezer. Thaw in the fridge overnight, or a warm bowl of water for about 20 minutes, before transferring to the oven and baking as directed.*

Dairy-Free Modifications: *Recipe is dairy-free when served with dairy-free sides.*

Gluten-Free Modifications: *Recipe is gluten-free when you use gluten-free soy and sweet Thai chili sauces.*

4. Buffalo Chicken Nachos

Yield: 4 servings
Active Time: 10 minutes . Cook Time: 8 hours in slow cooker

Recipe is written to make a single meal. Assembly Prep Directions & Shopping Lists will both contain directions and ingredients to make 2 meals, based on the number of servings you selected.

** This ingredient is used on the day you cook this meal. It is not added at the time you assemble and prepare your meals for the freezer.

Ingredients for Single Meal

- 4 - small boneless chicken breasts
- 1 - packet(s) ranch dressing mix
- 1 - cup(s) buffalo wing sauce
- 1 - bag(s) tortilla chips**
- 2 - cup(s) shredded mozzarella cheese**
- Garnish: - crumbled blue cheese**
- Garnish: - chopped celery**
- Side: - fruit**
- 1 - gallon-size freezer baggie(s)

Cooking Directions for Single Meal

1. Place the chicken breasts in the base of the slow cooker and sprinkle the ranch dressing mix over the top. Pour the buffalo wing sauce over the top.
2. Set on low and cook for 8 hours. Once the chicken is cooked, shred with 2 forks and combine with the sauce.
3. Preheat the oven to 400 F.
4. Assemble the nachos on baking sheet with tortilla chips, shredded buffalo chicken and shredded mozzarella cheese on top. Bake in the preheated oven for 10-15 minutes, or until cheese has melted.
5. Prepare fruit.
6. Serve Buffalo Chicken Nachos with crumbled blue cheese and chopped celery garnish, and side of fruit.

Assembly Prep Directions for 2 Meals

To each gallon-size plastic freezer baggie, add the following ingredients:

- 4 boneless chicken breasts
- 1 packet Ranch dressing mix
- 1 cup buffalo wing sauce

Remove as much air as possible and seal. Add label to baggie and freeze.

Freeze & Thaw Instructions: *Put baggie in the freezer and freeze up to 6 months in fridge freezer or 12 months in a deep freezer. Thaw in the fridge overnight, or a warm bowl of water for about 20 minutes, before transferring to the slow cooker and cooking on low for 8 hours. Shred the chicken once it is cooked, and then assemble the nachos as directed.*

Dairy-Free Modifications: *Recipe is dairy-free when served with dairy-free sides.*

Gluten-Free Modifications: *Recipe is gluten-free if you use gluten-free Ranch dressing mix.*

5. Slow Cooker BBQ Chicken Street Tacos

Yield: 4 servings
Active Time: 10 minutes . Cook Time: 8 hours in slow cooker

Recipe is written to make a single meal. Assembly Prep Directions & Shopping Lists will both contain directions and ingredients to make 2 meals, based on the number of servings you selected.

** This ingredient is used on the day you cook this meal. It is not added at the time you assemble and prepare your meals for the freezer.

Ingredients for Single Meal

- 4 - small boneless chicken breasts
- 2 - cup(s) BBQ sauce
- 1 - 15 oz. can(s) black beans
- 1 - red onion(s)
- 12 - corn tortillas**
- Garnish: - shredded cheddar cheese**
- Garnish: - chopped cilantro**
- Side: - fruit**
- 1 - gallon-size freezer baggie(s)

Cooking Directions for Single Meal

1. Chop the red onion.
2. Open, drain and rinse the can(s) of black beans.
3. Spray bottom of slow cooker with cooking spray. Add the chicken breasts, black beans, red onions and pour the BBQ sauce over the top. Add about 1/4 to 1/2 cup of water to thin out the sauce.
4. Set the slow cooker on low and cook for 8 hours. Once cooked, shred the chicken into the BBQ sauce. Spoon shredded chicken and sauce into the corn tortillas and top with garnishes.
5. Prepare fruit and garnishes.
6. Serve BBQ Chicken Street Tacos with side of fruit.

Assembly Prep Directions for 2 Meals

Chop 2 red onions.

Open, drain and rinse 2 cans of black beans.

To each gallon-size plastic freezer baggie, add the following ingredients:
- 4 small boneless chicken breasts
- 1 - 15 oz. can black beans
- Half of the chopped red onion
- 2 cups BBQ sauce

Remove as much air as possible and seal. Add label to baggie and freeze.

Freeze & Thaw Instructions: *Put baggie in the freezer and freeze up to 6 months in fridge freezer or 12 months in a deep freezer. Thaw in the fridge overnight, or a warm bowl of water for about 20 minutes, before adding contents of the baggie to the slow cooker with amount of water listed in the recipe. Set on low and cook for 8 hours. Shred the chicken and make tacos.*

Dairy-Free Modifications: *Recipe is dairy-free when shredded cheese garnish is omitted.*

Gluten-Free Modifications: *Recipe is gluten-free when served with gluten-free sides.*

Complete Shopping List by Recipe

1. Slow Cooker Ranch Chicken Tacos

- ☐ 8 - small boneless chicken breasts
- ☐ 1 - cup(s) chicken stock
- ☐ 2 - packet(s) ranch dressing mix
- ☐ 2 - packet(s) taco seasoning
- ☐ - Salt and pepper
- ☐ 16 - flour tortillas
- ☐ - coleslaw
- ☐ - Ranch salad dressing
- ☐ - salad
- ☐ 2 - gallon-size freezer baggie(s)

2. Slow Cooker Garlic Parmesan Chicken

- ☐ 8 - small boneless chicken breasts
- ☐ 4 - lb(s) baby potatoes
- ☐ 6 - Tbsp melted butter
- ☐ 8 - tsp minced garlic
- ☐ 2 - tsp dried thyme
- ☐ - Salt and pepper
- ☐ - shredded Parmesan cheese
- ☐ - veggies
- ☐ 2 - gallon-size freezer baggie(s)

3. Baked Sweet Chili Chicken

- ☐ 8 - small boneless chicken breasts
- ☐ - Salt and pepper
- ☐ 2 - cup(s) sweet Thai chili sauce
- ☐ 6 - Tbsp soy sauce
- ☐ - rice
- ☐ - veggies
- ☐ 2 - 9x13 disposable foil tray(s)

4. Buffalo Chicken Nachos

- ☐ 8 - small boneless chicken breasts
- ☐ 2 - packet(s) ranch dressing mix
- ☐ 2 - cup(s) buffalo wing sauce
- ☐ 2 - bag(s) tortilla chips
- ☐ 4 - cup(s) shredded mozzarella cheese
- ☐ - crumbled blue cheese
- ☐ - chopped celery
- ☐ - fruit
- ☐ 2 - gallon-size freezer baggie(s)

5. BBQ Chicken Street Tacos

- ☐ 8 - small boneless chicken breasts
- ☐ 4 - cup(s) BBQ sauce
- ☐ 2 - 15 oz. can(s) black beans
- ☐ 2 - red onion(s)
- ☐ 24 - corn tortillas
- ☐ - shredded cheddar cheese
- ☐ - chopped cilantro
- ☐ - fruit
- ☐ 2 - gallon-size freezer baggie(s)

Complete Shopping List by Store Section/Category

Meat

- ☐ 40 small boneless chicken breasts

Produce

- ☐ **Garnish:** chopped celery
- ☐ **Side:** fruit
- ☐ 4 lb(s) baby potatoes
- ☐ **Side:** veggies
- ☐ 2 red onion(s)
- ☐ **Garnish:** chopped cilantro
- ☐ **Garnish:** coleslaw
- ☐ **Side:** salad

Pantry Staples - Canned, Boxed

- ☐ 2 15 oz. can(s) black beans
- ☐ 1 cup(s) chicken stock
- ☐ **Side:** rice

Starchy Sides

- ☐ 24 corn tortillas
- ☐ 16 flour tortillas

Sauces/Condiments

- ☐ 2 cup(s) buffalo wing sauce
- ☐ 4 cup(s) BBQ sauce
- ☐ **Garnish:** Ranch salad dressing
- ☐ 2 cup(s) sweet Thai chili sauce
- ☐ 6 Tbsp soy sauce

Spices

- ☐ 4 packet(s) ranch dressing mix
- ☐ 8 tsp minced garlic
- ☐ 2 tsp dried thyme
- ☐ Salt and pepper
- ☐ 2 packet(s) taco seasoning

Dairy/Frozen

- ☐ 4 cup(s) shredded mozzarella cheese
- ☐ **Garnish:** crumbled blue cheese
- ☐ **Garnish:** shredded Parmesan cheese
- ☐ shredded cheddar cheese

Supplies

- ☐ 2 bag(s) tortilla chips
- ☐ **Side:** 8 gallon-size freezer baggie(s)
- ☐ 6 Tbsp melted butter
- ☐ **Side:** 2 9x13 disposable foil tray(s)

Freezer Meal Prep Day Shopping List by Recipe

Note: This shopping list doesn't include any side dish items like rice, dinner rolls, veggies or salad.

**In addition to a shopping list for prep day, this list could be used to help you organize ingredients on your counter before you begin preparing the meals for the freezer.

1. Slow Cooker Ranch Chicken Tacos

- ☐ 8 small boneless chicken breasts
- ☐ 1 cup(s) chicken stock
- ☐ 2 packet(s) ranch dressing mix
- ☐ 2 packet(s) taco seasoning
- ☐ Salt and pepper
- ☐ 2 gallon-size freezer baggie(s)

2. Slow Cooker Garlic Parmesan Chicken

- ☐ 8 small boneless chicken breasts
- ☐ 4 lb(s) baby potatoes
- ☐ 6 Tbsp melted butter
- ☐ 8 tsp minced garlic
- ☐ 2 tsp dried thyme
- ☐ Salt and pepper
- ☐ 2 gallon-size freezer baggie(s)

3. Baked Sweet Chili Chicken

- ☐ 8 small boneless chicken breasts
- ☐ Salt and pepper
- ☐ 2 cup(s) sweet Thai chili sauce
- ☐ 6 Tbsp soy sauce
- ☐ 2 9x13 disposable foil tray(s)

4. Buffalo Chicken Nachos

- ☐ 8 small boneless chicken breasts
- ☐ 2 packet(s) ranch dressing mix
- ☐ 2 cup(s) buffalo wing sauce
- ☐ 2 gallon-size freezer baggie(s)

5. BBQ Chicken Street Tacos

- ☐ 8 small boneless chicken breasts
- ☐ 4 cup(s) BBQ sauce
- ☐ 2 15 oz. can(s) black beans
- ☐ 2 red onion(s)
- ☐ 2 gallon-size freezer baggie(s)

Freezer Meal Prep Day Shopping List by Store Section/Category

Note: *This shopping list doesn't include any side dish items like fruit, dinner rolls, veggies or salad.*

Meat

- ☐ 40 small boneless chicken breasts

Produce

- ☐ 4 lb(s) baby potatoes
- ☐ 2 red onion(s)

Pantry Staples - Canned, Boxed

- ☐ 2 15 oz. can(s) black beans
- ☐ 1 cup(s) chicken stock

Sauces/Condiments

- ☐ 2 cup(s) buffalo wing sauce
- ☐ 4 cup(s) BBQ sauce
- ☐ 2 cup(s) sweet Thai chili sauce
- ☐ 6 Tbsp soy sauce

Spices

- ☐ 4 packet(s) ranch dressing mix
- ☐ 8 tsp minced garlic
- ☐ 2 tsp dried thyme

Salt and pepper

- ☐ 2 packet(s) taco seasoning

Supplies

- ☐ 6 Tbsp melted butter

Meal Assembly Instructions

☐ Label your bags/foil with printable labels or sharpie.
☐ Pull out all the ingredients into a central location or into stations.

Pre-Cook & Chop Instructions

☐ Chop 2 red onions.
☐ Melt 6 Tbsp butter and then stir in 8 tsp minced garlic and 2 tsp dried thyme.
☐ In a small mixing bowl, whisk together 2 cups sweet Thai chili sauce and 6 Tbsp soy sauce.
☐ Open, drain and rinse 2 cans of black beans.

The Assembly Prep should take between 30 to 35 minutes.

Assembly by Recipe (Set Out on the Counter)

If you prefer to load your freezer baggies and trays one recipe at a time, you can follow the below instructions.

Slow Cooker Ranch Chicken Tacos

To each gallon-size plastic freezer baggie, add the following ingredients:
- 4 boneless chicken breasts
- 1/2 cup chicken stock
- 1 packet Ranch dressing mix
- 1 packet taco seasoning
- Salt and pepper

Remove as much air as possible and seal. Add label to baggie and freeze.

Slow Cooker Garlic Parmesan Chicken

To each gallon-size plastic freezer baggie, add the following ingredients:
- 4 boneless chicken breasts
- 1 - 2 lb. bag baby potatoes
- Half of the melted butter sauce

Remove as much air as possible and seal. Add label to baggie and freeze.

Baked Sweet Chili Chicken

To each disposable tray, add the following ingredients:
- 4 small boneless chicken breasts
- Salt and pepper onto the chicken
- Half of the prepared sauce, directly on the chicken

Cover with foil or lid, add label and freeze.

Buffalo Chicken Nachos

To each gallon-size plastic freezer baggie, add the following ingredients:
- 4 boneless chicken breasts
- 1 packet Ranch dressing mix
- 1 cup buffalo wing sauce

Remove as much air as possible and seal. Add label to baggie and freeze.

BBQ Chicken Street Tacos

To each gallon-size plastic freezer baggie, add the following ingredients:
- 4 small boneless chicken breasts
- 1 - 15 oz. can black beans
- Half of the chopped red onion
- 2 cups BBQ sauce

Remove as much air as possible and seal. Add label to baggie and freeze.

Chapter 6 -
Freezer Meal Plan #2

5-Ingredient Chili
Classic Spaghetti Sauce
Cheesy Hamburger Helper
Cheddar Bacon Burgers
Skillet Nacho Dip

1. 5-Ingredient Chili

Yield: 4 servings
Active Time: 10 minutes . Cook Time: 20 minutes

Recipe is written to make a single meal. Assembly Prep Directions & Shopping Lists will both contain directions and ingredients to make 2 meals, based on the number of servings you selected.

** This ingredient is used on the day you cook this meal. It is not added at the time you assemble and prepare your meals for the freezer.

Ingredients for Single Meal

- 1 - lb(s) ground beef
- 1 - small white onion(s)
- 2 - 15 oz. can(s) red kidney beans
- 2 - 15 oz diced tom & green chile
- 2 - Tbsp chili powder
- - Salt and pepper
- - shredded cheese**
- Side: - salad**
- 1 - gallon-size freezer baggie(s)

Cooking Directions for Single Meal

1. Dice the onion.
2. Open and drain the 2 cans of red kidney beans. Open 2 cans diced tomatoes with green chiles.
3. In a large saucepan, brown the ground beef with salt and pepper. Drain and return to saucepan. Stir in the diced tomatoes with green chiles, drained red kidney beans, and 1 cup of hot water. Stir in the diced onion and chili powder. Bring to bubbling and reduce heat and simmer for 10 minutes to allow flavors to mingle.
4. Prepare the salad.
5. Serve 5-Ingredient Chili with shredded cheese garnish and salad.

Assembly Prep Directions for 2 Meals

Dice onions.

Brown 2 lbs. ground beef.

Open and drain 4 cans of red kidney beans.

Open 4 cans of diced tomatoes with green chiles.

To each gallon-size plastic freezer baggie, add the following ingredients:
- Half of the browned ground beef
- Half of the drained red kidney beans
- Half of the diced tomatoes with green chiles
- Half of the diced onion
- 2 Tbsp chili powder
- Salt and pepper

Remove as much air as possible and seal. Add label to baggie and freeze.

Freeze & Thaw Instructions: *Put baggie in the freezer and freeze up to 6 months in fridge freezer or 12 months in a deep freezer. Thaw in the fridge overnight, or a warm bowl of water for about 20 minutes, before transferring to a saucepan with 1 cup of water and reheating.*

Dairy-Free Modifications: *Omit cheese garnish for dairy- free meal.*

Gluten-Free Modifications: *Recipe is gluten-free when served with gluten-free sides.*

2. Classic Spaghetti Sauce

Yield: 4 servings
Active Time: 10 minutes . Cook Time: 20 minutes

Recipe is written to make a single meal. Assembly Prep Directions & Shopping Lists will both contain directions and ingredients to make 2 meals, based on the number of servings you selected.

** This ingredient is used on the day you cook this meal. It is not added at the time you assemble and prepare your meals for the freezer.

Ingredients for Single Meal

- 1 - lb(s) ground beef
- 1/2 - small white onion(s)
- 1 - 26 oz. jar(s) spaghetti sauce
- 2 - whole carrots
- 1 - small zucchini
- - Salt and pepper
- Side: - small shell pasta**
- Side: - veggies**
- 1 - gallon-size freezer baggie(s)

Cooking Directions for Single Meal

1. Cook pasta as directed.
2. In a large skillet, brown the ground beef with the chopped onion. Drain and return to skillet.
3. Stir in the spaghetti sauce, grated carrots and grated zucchini and simmer. Season with salt and pepper to taste.
4. Serve Classic Spaghetti Sauce with pasta and veggies.

Assembly Prep Directions for 2 Meals

Brown and drain 2 lbs. ground beef.

Chop 1 small white onion.

Peel and shred 4 whole carrots

Shred 2 zucchini.

To each gallon-size plastic freezer baggie, add the following ingredients:
- Half of the ground beef, browned and cooled
- Half of the chopped onions
- 26 oz. jar spaghetti sauce
- Half of the peeled and grated carrots
- Half of the grated zuchinni
- Salt and pepper

Remove as much air as possible and seal. Add label to baggie and freeze.

Freeze & Thaw Instructions: *Put baggie in the freezer and freeze up to 6 months in fridge freezer or 12 months in a deep freezer. Thaw in the fridge overnight, or a warm bowl of water for about 20 minutes, before transferring to saucepan.*

Dairy-Free Modifications: *Recipe is dairy-free when served with dairy-free sides.*

Gluten-Free Modifications: *Use gluten-free noodles. Sauce is gluten-free.*

3. Cheesy Hamburger Helper

Yield: 4 servings
Active Time: 15 minutes . Cook Time: 30 minutes

Recipe is written to make a single meal. Assembly Prep Directions & Shopping Lists will both contain directions and ingredients to make 2 meals, based on the number of servings you selected.

** This ingredient is used on the day you cook this meal. It is not added at the time you assemble and prepare your meals for the freezer.

Ingredients for Single Meal

- 1 - lb(s) ground beef
- 1 - Tbsp minced onion
- 1 - tsp garlic powder
- 1 - 15 oz. can(s) tomato sauce
- 1 - Tbsp Italian seasoning
- 12 - oz. pasta**
- 2 - cup(s) beef stock**
- - Salt and pepper
- 2 - cup(s) shredded mild cheddar cheese**
- Side: - veggies**
- 1 - gallon-size freezer baggie(s)

Cooking Directions for Single Meal

1. Open the cans of tomato sauce.
2. In a large skillet, brown the ground beef with the minced onion and garlic powder. Drain and return to skillet. Stir in the tomato sauce and Italian seasoning, and bring to bubbling. Then pour in the pasta and the beef stock.
3. Press the pasta into the beef stock, cover and simmer over medium low heat for 10 minutes, or until pasta is softened.
4. Remove from heat immediately to keep pasta from overcooking. Season with salt and pepper to taste. Sprinkle shredded cheese over the beef-pasta mixture.
5. Prepare veggies.
6. Serve Cheesy Hamburger Helper with veggies.

Assembly Prep Directions for 2 Meals

Brown 2 lbs. ground beef with 2 Tbsp minced onion and 2 tsp garlic powder. Let cool.

Open 2 cans of tomato sauce.

To each gallon-size plastic freezer baggie, add the following ingredients:
- Half of the browned ground beef
- 1 - 15 oz. can tomato sauce
- Salt and pepper
- 1 Tbsp Italian seasoning

Remove as much air as possible and seal. Add label to baggie and freeze.

Freeze & Thaw Instructions: *Put baggie in the freezer and freeze up to 6 months in fridge freezer or 12 months in a deep freezer. Thaw in the fridge overnight, or a warm bowl of water for about 20 minutes, before transferring to a large skillet and reheating. Once bubbling, add the pasta and beef stock, cover and simmer for 10 minutes, or until pasta is cooked. Top with shredded cheese before serving.*

Dairy-Free Modifications: *Unfortunately, there is not a great dairy-free option for this meal.*

Gluten-Free Modifications: *Recipe is gluten-free when made with gluten-free pasta.*

4. Cheddar Bacon Burgers

Yield: 4 servings
Active Time: 10 minutes . Cook Time: 10 minutes

Recipe is written to make a single meal. Assembly Prep Directions & Shopping Lists will both contain directions and ingredients to make 2 meals, based on the number of servings you selected.

** This ingredient is used on the day you cook this meal. It is not added at the time you assemble and prepare your meals for the freezer.

Ingredients for Single Meal

- 1 - lb(s) ground beef
- 1/2 - cup(s) bacon crumbles
- 1/2 - small white onion(s)
- 1 - tsp minced garlic
- 1 - tsp salt
- 4 - Tbsp BBQ sauce**
- 4 - hamburger buns**
- 4 - slices shredded sharp cheddar cheese**
- Side: - chips**
- Side: - fruit**
- 1 - gallon-size freezer baggie(s)

Cooking Directions for Single Meal

1. Preheat the grill.
2. Grate the onion with a cheese grater.
3. Combine the ground beef, bacon crumbles, BBQ sauce, grated onion (with juices), minced garlic and salt in a medium mixing bowl. Form into 4 patties.
4. Place the patties on the grill tray or veggie basket. See note about ways to keep patties together when grilling. Grill for 5 to 6 minutes per side, or until internal temperature should reach 165 F. If you need to cook the patties a little longer then you can move them to a cool part of the grill until they're cooked to your liking.
5. Once cooked, top with sliced sharp cheddar cheese. Add other favorite burger fixins.
6. Serve Cheddar Bacon Burgers with fruit and chips.

Assembly Prep Directions for 2 Meals

Grate 1 small white onion with cheese grater.

Combine 2 lbs. ground beef, 1 cup bacon crumbles, 8 Tbsp BBQ sauce, the grated onion (with juices), 2 tsp minced garlic, and 2 tsp salt in a medium mixing bowl. Form into 8 patties.

To each gallon-size plastic freezer baggie, add the following ingredients:
- 4 burger patties
- Foil between patties, if needed

Remove as much air as possible and seal. Add label to baggie and freeze.

Freeze & Thaw Instructions: *Put baggie in the freezer and freeze up to 6 months in fridge freezer or 12 months in a deep freezer. Thaw in the fridge overnight, or a warm bowl of water for about 20 minutes, before transferring to the grill and grilling as directed.*

Special Notes: *If you don't have a tray for your grill, put the patties in the freezer for 30 minutes to help them firm up and hold together better when grilling. Or you could grill them from partially frozen. Alternative cooking method: wrap the patties tightly in foil and place them in a 350 F oven for about 5 – 10 minutes until the desired temperature is reached.*

Dairy-Free Modifications: *Omit the cheese slices for dairy- free meal.*

Gluten-Free Modifications: *Recipe is gluten-free when served with gluten-free bun or in lettuce wrap.*

5. Skillet Nacho Dip

Yield: 4 servings
Active Time: 10 minutes . Cook Time: 20 minutes

Recipe is written to make a single meal. Assembly Prep Directions & Shopping Lists will both contain directions and ingredients to make 2 meals, based on the number of servings you selected.

** This ingredient is used on the day you cook this meal. It is not added at the time you assemble and prepare your meals for the freezer.

Ingredients for Single Meal

- 1 - lb(s) ground beef
- 2 - Tbsp minced onion
- 1 - tsp garlic powder
- 1 - 15 oz. can pinto beans
- 1 - 10 oz diced tom & green chile
- 1 packet - taco seasoning
- 2 - cup(s) shredded cheddar cheese**
- 1 - bag(s) tortilla chips**
- Garnish: - red bell pepper(s)**
- Garnish: - avocado(s)**
- Side: - salad**
- 1 - gallon-size freezer baggie(s)

Cooking Directions for Single Meal

1. Open, drain and rinse the pinto beans. Open the diced tomatoes with green chiles.
2. In a large skillet, brown the ground beef with the minced onion and garlic powder. Drain and return to the skillet. Stir in the rinsed pinto beans, diced tomatoes with green chilies, and taco seasoning. Combine well and bring to bubbling over medium low heat.
3. Just before serving, sprinkle the shredded cheddar cheese over the top and let melt. Top with bite size pieces of red bell pepper and avocado. Use tortilla chips to scoop up and eat the "nacho dip."
4. Prepare the salad.
5. Serve Skillet Nacho Dip with salad.

Assembly Prep Directions for 2 Meals

Brown 2 lbs. ground beef with 4 Tbsp minced onion and 2 tsp garlic powder. Drain and set aside to cool.

Open, drain and rinse 2 cans of pinto beans. Open 2 cans of diced tomatoes with green chiles.

To each gallon-size plastic freezer baggie, add the following ingredients:
- Half of the browned ground beef
- 1 - 15 oz. can pinto beans
- 1 - 10 oz. can diced tomatoes with green chiles
- 1 packet taco seasoning
- Salt and pepper

Remove as much air as possible and seal. Add label to baggie and freeze.

Freeze & Thaw Instructions: *Put baggie in the freezer and freeze up to 6 months in fridge freezer or 12 months in a deep freezer. Thaw in the fridge overnight, or a warm bowl of water for about 20 minutes, before transferring to the skillet to reheat and then top with shredded cheese and red pepper and avocado garnishes.*

Special Notes: *Use 2 Tbsp homemade taco seasoning in place of the packet of taco seasoning.*

Dairy-Free Modifications: *Omit cheese for dairy-free meal.*

Gluten-Free Modifications: *Recipe is gluten-free when served with gluten-free sides.*

Complete Shopping List by Recipe

1. 5-Ingredient Chili

- ☐ 2 - lb(s) ground beef
- ☐ 2 - small white onion(s)
- ☐ 2x2 - 15 oz. can(s) red kidney beans
- ☐ 4 - 15 oz diced tom & green chile
- ☐ 4 - Tbsp chili powder
- ☐ - Salt and pepper
- ☐ - shredded cheese
- ☐ - salad
- ☐ 2 - gallon-size freezer baggie(s)

2. Classic Spaghetti Sauce

- ☐ 2 - lb(s) ground beef
- ☐ 1 - small white onion(s)
- ☐ 2 - 26 oz. jar(s) spaghetti sauce
- ☐ 4 - whole carrots
- ☐ 2 - small zucchini
- ☐ - Salt and pepper
- ☐ - small shell pasta
- ☐ - veggies
- ☐ 2 - gallon-size freezer baggie(s)

3. Cheesy Hamburger Helper

- ☐ 2 - lb(s) ground beef
- ☐ 2 - Tbsp minced onion
- ☐ 2 - tsp garlic powder
- ☐ 2 - 15 oz. can(s) tomato sauce
- ☐ 2 - Tbsp Italian seasoning
- ☐ 24 - oz. pasta
- ☐ 4 - cup(s) beef stock
- ☐ - Salt and pepper
- ☐ 4 - cup(s) shredded mild cheddar cheese
- ☐ - veggies
- ☐ 2 - gallon-size freezer baggie(s)

4. Cheddar Bacon Burgers

- ☐ 2 - lb(s) ground beef
- ☐ 1 - cup(s) bacon crumbles
- ☐ 1 - small white onion(s)
- ☐ 2 - tsp minced garlic
- ☐ 2 - tsp salt
- ☐ 8 - Tbsp BBQ sauce
- ☐ 8 - hamburger buns
- ☐ 8 - slices shredded sharp cheddar cheese
- ☐ - chips
- ☐ - fruit
- ☐ 2 - gallon-size freezer baggie(s)

5. Skillet Nacho Dip

- ☐ 2 - lb(s) ground beef
- ☐ 4 - Tbsp minced onion
- ☐ 2 - tsp garlic powder
- ☐ 2 - 15 oz. can pinto beans
- ☐ 2 - 10 oz diced tom & green chile
- ☐ 2 - taco seasoning
- ☐ 4 - cup(s) shredded cheddar cheese
- ☐ 2 - bag(s) tortilla chips
- ☐ - red bell pepper(s)
- ☐ - avocado(s)
- ☐ - salad
- ☐ 2 - gallon-size freezer baggie(s)

Complete Shopping List by Store Section/Category

Meat

- ☐ 10 lb(s) ground beef
- ☐ 1 cup(s) bacon crumbles

Produce

- ☐ 4 small white onion(s)
- ☐ 4 whole carrots
- ☐ 2 small zucchini
- ☐ **Side:** veggies
- ☐ **Side:** salad
- ☐ **Garnish:** red bell pepper(s)
- ☐ **Garnish:** avocado(s)
- ☐ **Side:** fruit

Pantry Staples - Canned, Boxed

- ☐ **Side:** small shell pasta
- ☐ 2x2 15 oz. can(s) red kidney beans
- ☐ 4 15 oz diced tom & green chile
- ☐ 2 15 oz. can(s) tomato sauce
- ☐ 4 cup(s) beef stock
- ☐ 2 15 oz. can pinto beans
- ☐ 2 10 oz diced tom & green chile

Starchy Sides

- ☐ 24 oz. pasta
- ☐ 8 hamburger buns
- ☐ **Side:** chips

Sauces/Condiments

- ☐ 2 26 oz. jar(s) spaghetti sauce
- ☐ 8 Tbsp BBQ sauce

Spices

- ☐ Salt and pepper
- ☐ 4 Tbsp chili powder
- ☐ 6 Tbsp minced onion
- ☐ 4 tsp garlic powder
- ☐ 2 Tbsp Italian seasoning
- ☐ 2 taco seasoning
- ☐ 2 tsp minced garlic
- ☐ 2 tsp salt

Dairy/Frozen

- ☐ **Side:** shredded cheese
- ☐ 4 cup(s) shredded mild cheddar cheese
- ☐ 4 cup(s) shredded cheddar cheese
- ☐ 8 slices shredded sharp cheddar cheese

Supplies

- ☐ **Side:** 10 gallon-size freezer baggie(s)
- ☐ 2 bag(s) tortilla chips

Freezer Meal Prep Day Shopping List by Recipe

Note: *This shopping list doesn't include any side dish items like rice, dinner rolls, veggies or salad.*
**In addition to a shopping list for prep day, this list could be used to help you organize ingredients on your counter before you begin preparing the meals for the freezer.

1. 5-Ingredient Chili

- ☐ 2 lb(s) ground beef
- ☐ 2 small white onion(s)
- ☐ 2x2 15 oz. can(s) red kidney beans
- ☐ 4 15 oz diced tom & green chile
- ☐ 4 Tbsp chili powder
- ☐ Salt and pepper
- ☐ 2 gallon-size freezer baggie(s)

2. Classic Spaghetti Sauce

- ☐ 2 lb(s) ground beef
- ☐ 1 small white onion(s)
- ☐ 2 26 oz. jar(s) spaghetti sauce
- ☐ 4 whole carrots
- ☐ 2 small zucchini
- ☐ Salt and pepper
- ☐ 2 gallon-size freezer baggie(s)

3. Cheesy Hamburger Helper

- ☐ 2 lb(s) ground beef
- ☐ 2 Tbsp minced onion
- ☐ 2 tsp garlic powder
- ☐ 2 15 oz. can(s) tomato sauce
- ☐ 2 Tbsp Italian seasoning
- ☐ Salt and pepper
- ☐ 2 gallon-size freezer baggie(s)

4. Cheddar Bacon Burgers

- ☐ 2 lb(s) ground beef
- ☐ 1 cup(s) bacon crumbles
- ☐ 1 small white onion(s)
- ☐ 2 tsp minced garlic
- ☐ 2 tsp salt
- ☐ 2 gallon-size freezer baggie(s)

5. Skillet Nacho Dip

- ☐ 2 lb(s) ground beef
- ☐ 4 Tbsp minced onion
- ☐ 2 tsp garlic powder
- ☐ 2 15 oz. can pinto beans
- ☐ 2 10 oz diced tom & green chile
- ☐ 2 taco seasoning
- ☐ 2 gallon-size freezer baggie(s)

Freezer Meal Prep Day Shopping List by Store Section/Category

Note: *This shopping list doesn't include any side dish items like fruit, dinner rolls, veggies or salad.*

Meat

- ☐ 10 lb(s) ground beef
- ☐ 1 cup(s) bacon crumbles

Produce

- ☐ 4 small white onion(s)
- ☐ 4 whole carrots
- ☐ 2 small zucchini

Pantry Staples - Canned, Boxed

- ☐ 2x2 15 oz. can(s) red kidney beans
- ☐ 4 15 oz diced tom & green chile
- ☐ 2 15 oz. can(s) tomato sauce
- ☐ 2 15 oz. can pinto beans
- ☐ 2 10 oz diced tom & green chile

Sauces/Condiments

- ☐ 2 26 oz. jar(s) spaghetti sauce

Spices

- ☐ Salt and pepper
- ☐ 4 Tbsp chili powder
- ☐ 6 Tbsp minced onion
- ☐ 4 tsp garlic powder
- ☐ 2 Tbsp Italian seasoning
- ☐ 2 taco seasoning
- ☐ 2 tsp minced garlic
- ☐ 2 tsp salt

Meal Assembly Instructions

- ☐ Label your bags/foil with printable labels or sharpie.
- ☐ Pull out all the ingredients into a central location or into stations.

Pre-Cook & Chop Instructions

- ☐ Brown 2 lbs. ground beef with 2 Tbsp minced onion and 2 tsp garlic powder. Let cool.
- ☐ Dice onions.
- ☐ Brown 2 lbs. ground beef.
- ☐ Brown and drain 2 lbs. ground beef.
- ☐ Brown 2 lbs. ground beef with 4 Tbsp minced onion and 2 tsp garlic powder. Drain and set aside to cool.
- ☐ Chop 1 small white onion.
- ☐ Peel and shred 4 whole carrots
- ☐ Shred 2 zucchini.
- ☐ Grate 1 small white onion with cheese grater.
- ☐ Combine 2 lbs. ground beef, 1 cup bacon crumbles, 8 Tbsp BBQ sauce, the grated onion (with juices), 2 tsp
- ☐ minced garlic, and 2 tsp salt in a medium mixing bowl. Form into 8 patties.
- ☐ Open 2 cans of tomato sauce.
- ☐ Open and drain 4 cans of red kidney beans.
- ☐ Open 4 cans of diced tomatoes with green chiles.
- ☐ Open, drain and rinse 2 cans of pinto beans.
- ☐ Open 2 cans of diced tomatoes with green chiles.

The Assembly Prep should take between 30 to 35 minutes.

Assembly by Recipe (Set Out on the Counter)

If you prefer to load your freezer baggies and trays one recipe at a time, you can follow the below instructions.

5-Ingredient Chili

To each gallon-size plastic freezer baggie, add the following ingredients:
- Half of the browned ground beef
- Half of the drained red kidney beans
- Half of the diced tomatoes with green chiles
- Half of the diced onion
- 2 Tbsp chili powder
- Salt and pepper

Remove as much air as possible and seal. Add label to baggie and freeze.

Classic Spaghetti Sauce

To each gallon-size plastic freezer baggie, add the following ingredients:
- Half of the ground beef, browned and cooled Half of the chopped onions
- 26 oz. jar spaghetti sauce
- Half of the peeled and grated carrots
- Half of the grated zuchinni
- Salt and pepper

Remove as much air as possible and seal. Add label to baggie and freeze.

Cheesy Hamburger Helper

To each gallon-size plastic freezer baggie, add the following ingredients:
- Half of the browned ground beef
- 1 - 15 oz. can tomato sauce
- Salt and pepper
- 1 Tbsp Italian seasoning

Remove as much air as possible and seal. Add label to baggie and freeze.

Cheddar Bacon Burgers

To each gallon-size plastic freezer baggie, add the following ingredients:
- 4 burger patties
- Foil between patties, if needed

Remove as much air as possible and seal. Add label to baggie and freeze.

Skillet Nacho Dip

To each gallon-size plastic freezer baggie, add the following ingredients:
- Half of the browned ground beef
- 1 - 15 oz. can pinto beans
- 1 - 10 oz. can diced tomatoes with green chiles
- 1 packet taco seasoning
- Salt and pepper

Remove as much air as possible and seal. Add label to baggie and freeze.

Freezer Cooking Resources
from Erin Chase

Let's Connect

Hi friend! Need more help or inspiration on your f reezer cooking journey? Come join our group on Facebook - it's basically a "freezer cooking hotline" and an amazing, supportive community.
Visit https://bit.ly/MyFrEZFB to join the group.

Join MyFreezEasy

Freezer Meal Cookbooks

Freezer Meal Plan PDFs

Made in the USA
Columbia, SC
10 September 2024

42037777R00059